# FASTING IN ISLAM

ISLAM IN PRACTICE

A COMPREHENSIVE GUIDE

# FASTING IN ISLAM

Ali Budak

TUGHRA BOOKS
New Jersey

Originally published in Turkish as Soru ve Cevaplarla Oruç in 2005.

25 24 23 22     4 5 6 7



Published by Tughra Books
335 Clifton Avenue, Clifton
New Jersey 07011, USA

www.tughrabooks.com

Library of Congress Cataloging-in-Publication Data Available

ISBN: 978-1-59784-919-7

# Table of Contents

CHAPTER 3
TYPES OF FASTS

# Introduction

Going back any time in history, the existence of religious thought can be traced in all communities and societies, even in the most primitive tribes.

In Islamic terminology, religion means "the set of Divine principles that guide humanity to what is good and right." Its message does not exclude any individual or any single being. Those people who choose to obey these Divine principles do so of their own free will. Religion exalts volition; humanity is advised to use their conscious inclination for good. This advice is not brought to bear with force; rather the free will of humanity is appealed to. The ultimate goal of religion is to lead people willingly to absolute and eternal happiness.

Religion guides humanity to what is good and right firstly through belief; this is the essence of religion. Through wisdom and reasoning a person can attain a degree of certainty in belief through direct observation of the truths of nature and discover that there is a Creator who created not only humanity but the entire universe as well.

However, true belief requires far more than the simple affirmation of reason. Belief in Allah can only be enjoyed fully when His Name is recited by and heard from the voice of Prophets who teach people the truth of things, inform them of their relationship with the universe, and thus support the voice of the conscience and the inward affirmation of the heart. Human beings, in this way, attain true guidance by following in the footsteps of the Prophets and by having, in the Messengers of Allah, the most sublime pattern of conduct so that they can look forward with hope to Allah the Almighty.

The strength and durability of such true belief and pure faith depend on worship. Acts of worship are shields and armor that protect faith from idleness and decay. Therefore, all believers should pray with their hearts, intellects, and bodies in order to nourish their faith. Worship is the most sublime way to demonstrate that Allah is the only deity to be worshipped and that human beings are His servants. Hence, acts of worship are the ways in which we reflect our knowledge of Him and harmonize the relationship of the creation with the Creator.

Another aspect of religion pertains to the interrelations of human beings in the ordinary course of life. True believers seek the pleasure of Allah in the arrangement of their relationships. Commercial transactions and ethics, for instance, need to be conducted by acting in His way. Those who carry out their actions mindful of Allah thus observe the laws of Allah in their commercial affairs and abide by these in their dealings with all they come into contact; such actions cause their mundane economic activities to be accepted as a form of worship. In this sense, all of their activities and their entire life are a form of worship as they submit themselves to the pleasure of Allah the Almighty.

Religion is a whole; it is the collection of Divine principles that engender various forms of worship. Those who accept some parts of religion while denying others lack sufficient knowledge of religion and do not recognize its true form. Religion is like a tree: issues concerning faith are its roots while those concerning worship are its branches and leaves. Following the same analogy, a polite manner and attitude in daily life is the flower of the tree, while the rules are fence that wards off harm, and prayers are the elements that give it sustenance. Religion, which displays such a wholeness and unity, has been completely established by the Almighty Allah and conveyed and taught to humanity by His Messengers. Likewise, just as all the interrelated and cooperative parts above go to make the integral whole of a tree, fasting as an act of worship is an essential part of the overall Divine set of principles.

This book seeks to explore the Divine institution of fasting by answering frequently asked questions. In this way, this comprehensive guide to fasting in Islam aims to make readers better understand and be more aware of this essential act of worship.

# Chapter 1
# What is Fasting?

## What is fasting in Islam?

The word sawm is the Arabic equivalent for fasting; it means to abstain. In the language used in the Qur'an and the records of Prophet Muhammad's sayings, peace and blessings be upon him, it signifies the conscious abstinence from the cravings of the carnal soul by willingly abstaining from food, drink, and sexual intercourse from the break of dawn until sunset in order to maintain spiritual discipline and self control.

Fasting was not ordained during the first years of Islam, but rather after the Messenger's emigration to Madina; this is true for many other religious precepts as well. To give an exact date, fasting was enjoined in Sha'ban (the eighth month in the Islamic calendar) of the second year after the Messenger's emigration to Madina.

Every religion or faith, be it divinely revealed or not, has prescribed precepts and interdicts for its followers.

The believers of a religion demonstrate sincerity and loyalty by practicing the teachings of that religion. Islam, a religion of Divine truth and justice, has enjoined certain ways of worship and behavior to its followers and made those followers responsible for fulfilling these acts of worship.

Observing the fast in the month of Ramadan (the ninth month in the Islamic calendar) is one of the five pillars of Islam; it is enjoined in the Qur'an, and is therefore obligatory. In the Qur'an, issues are handled in a general way. It is Prophet Muhammad who provides detailed explanations of the Islamic decrees mentioned in the Qur'an, for it is he who is the foremost and greatest interpreter of the Holy Book. Some evidence in the Qur'an and the Prophet's teachings that tell us fasting is compulsory are included in the following two sections, which present questions and answers concerning these matters.

## What is the Qur'anic evidence for the necessity of fasting?

Concerning the order to fast, the Qur'an declares:

يَا أَيُّهَا الَّذِينَ آمَنُوا كُتِبَ عَلَيْكُمُ الصِّيَامُ كَمَا
كُتِبَ عَلَى الَّذِينَ مِنْ قَبْلِكُمْ لَعَلَّكُمْ تَتَّقُونَ

(which means: "O, you who believe! Prescribed for you is the Fast, as it was prescribed for those before you, that you may deserve Allah's protection against the temptations of your carnal soul and attain piety" [al-Baqarah 2:183].)

شَهْرُ رَمَضَانَ الَّذِي أُنْزِلَ فِيهِ الْقُرْآنُ هُدًى لِلنَّاسِ وَبَيِّنَاتٍ مِنَ الْهُدَى وَالْفُرْقَانِ فَمَنْ شَهِدَ مِنْكُمُ الشَّهْرَ فَلْيَصُمْهُ وَمَنْ كَانَ مَرِيضًا أَوْ عَلَى سَفَرٍ فَعِدَّةٌ مِنْ أَيَّامٍ أُخَرَ يُرِيدُ اللَّهُ بِكُمُ الْيُسْرَ وَلَا يُرِيدُ بِكُمُ الْعُسْرَ وَلِتُكْمِلُوا الْعِدَّةَ وَلِتُكَبِّرُوا اللَّهَ عَلَى مَا هَدَاكُمْ وَلَعَلَّكُمْ تَشْكُرُونَ

(which means: "Ramadan is the month in which the Qur'an (began to be) revealed, providing guidance for human beings, with clear verses to guide and to distinguish right from wrong; therefore whoever witnesses that month shall fast it, and whoever is sick or on a journey, the same number of days which one did not observe fasts must be made up from other days. Allah desires ease and does not desire difficulty for you, that you may complete the total number of fasting days; glorify Him in that He has guided you and that you may give thanks" [al-Baqarah 2:185].)

## What do the Prophet's teachings say about the necessity of fasting?

The noble Prophet, peace and blessings be upon him, said: "Islam is built on five pillars; these are the testimony that there is no deity worthy of worship but Allah and the testimony that Muhammad is His Messenger, the establishment of the five Daily Prayers, the prescribed alms, observing the fast of Ramadan, and the pilgrimage to the House of Allah, Ka'ba, for those who are able."[1]

Another record of the Prophet's teachings concerning the compulsory nature of fasting during Ramadan is as follows:

> A man with unkempt hair came to the Messenger of Allah and said, "O Messenger of Allah! Inform me what Allah has made compulsory for me as regards the Prayers." He replied: "You have to offer the five Daily Prayers perfectly." He said: "Am I obliged to perform any other Prayer besides these?" The Prophet said: "No, except that which you observe voluntarily, out of your own free will." The man further asked, "Inform me what Allah has made compulsory for me as regards fasting." He replied, "You have to fast during the whole month of Ramadan." The inquirer said: "Am I obliged to fast anything else besides this?" The Prophet said: "No, except that which you observe out of your own free will." The man further asked, "Tell me how many alms Allah has enjoined on me." Thus, the Prophet informed him about all the pillars of Islam. The man then said, "By Him Who has honored you, I will neither make

---

1 al-Bukhari, Iman, 1; Muslim, Iman, 20; at-Tirmidhi, Iman, 3.

any addition to this, nor will I decrease anything out of it." Allah's Messenger remarked, "He is successful if he is truthful in what he affirms."2

## What is the history of fasting in world civilizations?

The practice of fasting has its origins in the earliest recorded religions. In spite of some differences associated with the practice of fasting in various belief systems, fasting as an institution for spiritual reasons is common to all religions and well established among the Jews and the Christians.

The life accounts of all the prophets in revealed scriptures and in popular knowledge who were recipients of divine commandments show that they were actually leading a holy way of life for a certain period of time, even before they started receiving Divine Guidance. During this period, they abstained from food, drink, and other human needs, and they enabled their souls to have communion with Allah and finally were rewarded with His revelation. The Bible mentions that Jesus, Moses, Daniel, Elijah, and David, peace be upon them, all fasted. Moses received the Law after fasting for forty days. Similarly, Jesus fasted for forty days in the wilderness before he was called to his ministry. Prophet David fasted every other day. This fast of David is one of the most virtuous of the recommended fasts in Islam as well. Pro-

---

[2] al-Bukhari, Iman, 3; Sawm, 1; Muslim, Iman, 8, 9; Abu Dawud, Salat, 1; an-Nasai, Salat, 4.

longed fasting was practiced by the Biblical saints, Ahab, Anna, Esther, Hannah, Ezra, John the Baptist, and the disciples.

Fasting is not only mentioned in the Bible, both Old and New Testament, but also in the Mahabharat of Hinduism, and in the Upanishads of India, as well as being observed among the Jains. The original significance of fasting as a form of spiritual devotion was the same among the nations and communities of such ancient world as the Celts, Aztecs, Babylonians, ancient Peruvians, and the Assyrians.

The Qur'an is the greatest evidence concerning the order of fasting prescribed for modern and ancient people alike:

> O, you who believe! Prescribed for you is the Fast, as it was prescribed for those before you, that you may deserve Allah's protection against the temptations of your carnal soul and attain piety (al-Baqarah 2:183).

## How is fasting observed in Judaism?

The Jewish equivalent for fasting is taanit. This word is derived from the Hebrew word ta'aanat, which means afflicting the carnal soul and distressing the body.

There are various fasts in Judaism. Yom Kippur, which is observed on the tenth of Tishri in the Jewish calendar, is the most important and firmly declared fast in the Torah. It is the holiest of all the festivals of Jewish creed and is known as the Day of Atonement. Followers of the Jewish faith repent for their sins and ask to be forgiven by Allah on this day.[3] This fast is expiation for idolizing the calf during the time of the Prophet Moses; believers fast on this day to thank Allah for pardoning them after worshipping the calf for their sins. In the evening of the ninth of Tishri, the first month of the Jewish calendar, those who fast eat and drink abundantly to prepare for the fast that begins on the same night and finishes on the evening of the next day when they see the first two stars in the sky. This means that the fast lasts about twenty-five hours. As their fasts are for the most part commemorations of hardship and symbols of grief, believers adopt a sorrowful appearance. Eating, drinking, washing or anointing the body, wearing leather shoes, and sexual relations are all forbidden during this time period.[4]

Followers of the Jewish faith are expected to lead a holy life by observing the fast and other forms of worship for long hours on Yom Kippur, which concludes the Ten Days of Repentance. During these days observant Jews repent for their sins.[5]

---

3 Kahraman, Ahmet, Dinler Tarihi (History of Religions), p. 145.

4 Olgun, Tahir, Müslümanlıkta İbadet Tarihi (History of Worship in Islam), p.125.

5 Çelebi, Ahmet, Mukayeseli Dinler Açısından Yahudilik (Judaism from a Comparative Perspective), p. 326, (Trans.: A. M. Büyükçınar, Ö. F. Harman).

It is reported that Prophet Moses promised that the Children of Israel would be given a book if their enemies were to be destroyed by Allah and that upon the destruction of the Pharaoh Moses prayed to Allah for the book to be sent. Allah the Almighty ordered him to fast for thirty days during the month of Dhu al-Qada, and then the first ten days of the following month, making a total number of forty days to be fasted. The first thirty days were devoted to asceticism and the restraint of the carnal desires in order to reach Allah and during the last ten days the Ten Commandments were revealed and the Prophet Moses spoke with Allah.[6] The fast Moses observed is recorded in the Old Testament as follows:

> And he was there with the Lord forty days and forty nights; he did neither eat bread, nor drink water. And he wrote upon the tables the words of the covenant, the Ten Commandments (Exodus 34:28).

Moreover, we learn from the Old Testament that after the exile of the Jews to Babylon, the Sons of Israel began to observe fasts on certain days of the year in order to commemorate some of the tragic events in their history. The fasts they observed took the Hebraic names of the months in which these events took place. Of these, the

---

6 Yazır, Elmalılı Hamdi, Hak Dini Kur'an Dili (Language of the Qur'an, the True Faith), 6/2275.

four regular fasts mentioned below commemorate the destruction of Jerusalem and other sorrowful events.[7]

1. The Fast of the Seventeenth of Tammuz is observed in commemoration of the first breach in the walls of Jerusalem during the Babylonian siege.
2. The Fast of the Ninth of Av is a major fast that lasts 25 hours in commemoration of the destruction of the first and second Jewish Temple, the Jewish expulsion from Spain, and other tragedies that have befallen the Jewish people.
3. The Fast of the Third of Tishri or the Fast of Gedaliah commemorates Gedaliah, who was murdered during the invasion of Jerusalem when he was the governor of Judea.
4. The Fast of the Tenth of Tevet is observed in commemoration of the beginning of the Babylonian siege of Jerusalem.

In addition to these fasts, observant Jews keep the following:[8]

1. The Fast of Esther (Adar 13)[9]
2. The Fast of the Firstborn Male (Nissan 14)

---

7 Olgun, pp. 125-126.

8 Al-Nadwi, Dört Rükün (The Four Pillars), p. 203.

9 See the Old Testament, Esther, 9:20-32.

3. The Fast of Erev Yom Kippur (the day before Yom Kippur)
4. The Fast of Sukkoth (The Festival of Tabernacles or Booths, Tishri 15)
5. The Fast of the Newlyweds
6. The Fast of Passover (Exodus from Egypt, Nissan 15)
7. The Fast of Rosh Hodesh (New Moon)
8. The Fast of Shavuot (special temple celebrations)
9. Fasts observed to protest strict commandments of rabbis.[10]

In Judaism a fast generally begins at dawn and finishes in the evening when the first two stars are seen in the sky. However, the fasts of Yom Kippur and the Ninth of Av (August) begin in the evening that precedes the day of the fast and finish the next evening. Jews are advised and encouraged to give alms, feed the poor, and donate food from the traditional dinners to others. In the first nine days of August and on some other days between the seventeenth of July and the tenth of August Jews observe partial-fasts during which it is forbidden for them to eat meat and drink alcoholic beverages.[11]

---

[10] Feyizli, Tahsin, İslam'da ve Diğer İnanç Sistemlerinde Oruç-Kurban (Fasting and Sacrifice in Islam and Other Belief Systems), pp. 25-27.

[11] Al-Nadwi, p. 203; Yazır, 2/183-185.

## How do Christians observe fasting?

Fasting is practiced to this day among Roman Catholics, Orthodox Christians, and in most Protestant denominations, in particular among the Episcopalians and Lutherans. Other Christian denominations do not observe specified times of fasting, for they see fasting as being a personal spiritual experience, not a rite that is prescribed as part of public worship.

The recommendations of Jesus concerning fasting are stated in the Bible:

> Whenever you fast, do not be like the hypocrites, with sad faces. For they disfigure their faces, that they may be seen by men to be fasting. Truly I say to you, they have their reward in full (Matthew 6:16).

Jesus is said to have fasted alone in the wilderness east of Jerusalem for forty days before he was called to his ministry. He is believed to have also fasted on the Day of Atonement, which is obligatory in Judaism. According to the Bible, he decreed no other rules concerning fasting.

Toward the end of the first century, a tendency to pass laws about fasting came about. Believers had formerly been given the choice to fast or not. Obviously, some monks and churches proposed a kind of fasting in order to restrain materialistic and carnal desires.

After the Reformation, the Anglican Church designated and defined the days that were to be fasted, but enjoined no other principles that those who were going to fast should follow. The form or manner of fasting was to be decided by the believers themselves.[12]

Today, fasting is observed in Roman and Eastern Orthodox Christianity on certain holy days, just as it is in other Christian sects.

For Roman Catholics, Ash Wednesday and Good Friday are still days of fasting and abstinence as specified in the Code of Canon Law for the rules of fasting adopted by the Ecumenical Council (cc. 1250-1253). On these two solemn days, Roman Catholics are enjoined to fast by partially reducing the size of their daily meals and abstaining from the consumption of meat.

For observant Orthodox Christians, fasting refers to abstention from animal products, oils, wine, and spirits. By fasting with prayer and almsgiving, they aim to come closer to God.

For many Protestants, among whom the spiritual disciplines have a growing importance, personal fasts take on different forms. These vary in the extent of the fast, from the exclusion of a single item to not consuming any food or beverage; and in the duration, from a single day up to and beyond forty days. The purposes of these fasts vary, including spiritual intervention in difficult circumstances, or to attain victory in a challenging personal

---

[12] Al-Nadwi, pp. 203-205; Yazır, 2/183-185.

area, but most often are intended to increase one's awareness and communion with Almighty God.

The Latter Day Saints, otherwise known as Mormons—who consider their faith to have its roots in Christianity but are generally understood to be following a completely new religion at the level of doctrine if not practice—are encouraged to fast for twenty-four hours once a month, and the first Sunday of the month is usually designated as a Fast Sunday. They consider fasting a way to focus on the spiritual experience.

## How do non-Abrahamic faiths practice fasting?

Fasting is not only mentioned in the Qur'an, the Gospel, and the Torah, but also in the Mahabharat of Hinduism and in the Upanishads of India as well as being observed among the ancient Greeks and the Egyptians.

In Hinduism, fasting is observed with the purpose of purifying the soul on fixed days of the year and during religious festivals. Every group in Hinduism has their own days for supplication and worship. On these days most Hindus do not eat, and they spend the whole night reading their holy books and meditating on God. There are some days on which only women observe fasting. Followers of Brahmanism fast on the eleventh and the twelfth days of the months of their calendar, which makes a total of twenty-four days a year. Buddhist monks and nuns fast each day after the noon meal, though many orders today do not enforce this fast. Jainism, an India-based faith, has stricter rules and regulations about fasting, and its followers fast for forty consecutive days to achieve passionless detachment from life and purify the soul.

In ancient Egypt fasting was observed on religious festivals. In the ancient history of Greece, only women used to fast on the second day of Thesmophoria, the Greek Festival of Thanksgiving. Commands and recommendations about fasting can even be found in the books of fire-worshippers.[13]

## How was fasting practiced among the pre-Islamic Arabs?

The pre-Islamic Arabs used to fast on the Day of Ashura, which is the tenth day of the month of Muharram. It is reported that Prophet Muhammad fasted on the Day of Ashura and ordered the believers to fast on this day; it is the day that Allah saved Moses and his followers from the Pharaoh, who was drowned in Red Sea along with his army.

According to Abdullah ibn Abbas, when Prophet Muhammad came to Madina, he saw the Jews fasting on the tenth of Muharram in celebration of Moses' victory

[13] Al-Nadwi, pp. 200-201.

over the Pharaoh. Upon seeing this, the Prophet fasted on Ashura day and ordered others to fast as well.[14]

According to another tradition reported by mother Aisha, the Prophet's wife, "The people of Quraysh used to fast on the day of Ashura in the pre-Islamic period, and then the Messenger of Allah ordered Muslims to fast on it till the fasting in the month of Ramadan was prescribed; whereupon the Prophet said, 'It is without a doubt that the Day of Ashura is one of Allah's days. From now on, who so wishes should fast on that day; who so wishes does not have to.' In this way, fasting on this day was left up to individual choice."[15]

## What is the importance of fasting in Islam?

Fasting in the month of Ramadan is one of the five pillars of Islam, and thus one of the most important acts of worship. Through fasting, a believer is able to draw closer to Allah by abandoning the things people enjoy, including food, drink, and sexual relations that are otherwise lawful in the ordinary course of life. Fasting makes the sincerity of one's faith and devotion to Allah all the more evident and thus, Allah will be pleased with the believers as they abandon worldly comforts for His sake, and He Himself will give the reward for this. The worship of fasting outweighs the

[14] Bukhari, Sawm 69; Muslim, Siyam 111, 112; Abu Dawud, Sawm 63.
[15] Bukhari, Sawm 69.

other forms of devotions in reward. It is so sacred an act of worship that no pen and paper can suffice to describe its merits and rewards; it is observed only to seek the pleasure of Allah the Almighty.

## What did the Prophet say about the significance of fasting?

As an immaculate bearer of Allah's final revelation to all people, Prophet Muhammad, peace and blessings be upon him, called everybody to fast during the month of Ramadan and set them a perfect example with his most sublime practice of fasting in his life; this is what believers try to emulate.

Abu Hurayra reported that Allah's Messenger emphasized the manifold rewards of observing the worship of fasting with sincerity:

> Allah said, "Every act of the humanity is for themselves, except fasting. It is for Me, and I shall reward it. That is because they abstain from food, drink and carnal desires for My sake." Fasting is a shield or protection from the fire and from committing sins. If one of you is fasting, they should avoid food and drink, sexual relations, and quarreling, and if somebody should fight or quarrel with them, they should say, "I am fasting." By Allah in Whose Hand my soul is, the unpleasant smell coming out from the mouth of a fasting person is better in the sight of Allah than the scent of

> musk. The one who fasts has two occasions of joy, one at the time of breaking their fast, and the other at the time when they will meet their Lord; then they will be pleased because of their fasting.[16]

The person who fasts should observe this sacred act of worship in the light of the Prophet's teachings; this is a school for the training of the spirit, the purification of the heart, and protection from committing sins. No matter whether one fasts only for a day or a month, they cut themselves off from worldly comforts at the behest of the Almighty Allah, Who shall give a reward for it. Allah has chosen fasting for Himself, and He will reward it and multiply the reward without measure. Fasting has a special quality that is not found in anything else and that is its close connection to Allah; this is, such that He says: "Fasting is for Me, and I shall reward it." These are the emotions with which fasting should be observed.

The unpleasant breath of the person fasting is caused by hunger. The Prophetic saying above gives the believer good news regarding the change in their breath, which is sweeter to the Almighty than musk. Angels, who are pure spirits, enjoy some kinds of odors. For example, they enjoy the sweet fragrance of roses, daffodils, musk, and amber. Such odors are like keys to the hidden treasures

---

16 al-Bukhari, Sawm 2; Muslim, Siyam 152; at-Tirmidhi, Sawm 54; an-Nasai, Siyam 41; Ibn Maja, Siyam 1.

of eternal worlds that we cannot perceive with our eyes. The breath of the person fasting is one of those sweet odors. The reason for this odor being perceived in this way is that it forms a private connection between the Creator and the creation. Thus, fasting has deep inner aspects along with its more obvious benefits and merits.

In another saying reported by Abu Hurayra the Prophet said: "There are alms for everything. Observing the fast is the alms of the body. Observing the fast is half of patience."[17] On another occasion he said: "Fasting is half of patience, and cleansing is half of faith."[18] From the saying of "Fasting is half of patience," it can be deduced that the other half of patience is allocated to the other issues of religion. It is clear that half of the religion is found in having the patience to carry out responsibilities concerning worship that were enjoined by Allah, the continuous determination to obey His commands, in not abandoning His gate, the gate to pure bliss, and in persevering in the avoidance of sins. While observing the fast, the believer not only restrains their carnal desires and hence shows a great resistance to sins, but also abstains from food and beverage, which is particularly difficult during the long hot days of summer, and thus exercises patience with worship. Therefore, fasting forms one fourth

---

17 at-Tirmidhi, Daawat 86; Ibn Maja, Siyam 44.

18 at-Tirmidhi, Daawat 85; Ibn Maja, Siyam 44; ad-Darimi, Wudu 2; Ibn Hanbal, Musnad 4/260.

of the religion. As is known, it is one of the five main pillars of Islam, the others being Daily Prayers, giving alms, and pilgrimage to the Ka'ba in Mecca, with the fifth being bearing witness with the tongue and heart that Allah is the only deity and that Muhammad is His Messenger.

Although everything done for the sake of Allah has a reward, none of the good deeds or acts of worship can be compared to fasting when it comes to Allah's pleasure and reward. Abu Umama reports:

> I asked the Messenger of Allah to tell me a religious practice I should perform. He said: "Observe the fast, since this unique act of worship has no equal." I repeated my question and he again said: "Observe the fast, since it has no equal." I asked the same question for the third time and he answered as he did before: "Observe the fast, since it has no equal."[19]

The Almighty Allah singles out fasting from all other types of worship because fasting has no equal. The fact that the believer is abstaining from food and drink both in public and in private shows their honest faith and strong love of Allah, their knowledge and feeling that Allah is All-Knowing. For this reason, the Almighty has made the reward for fasting greater than the reward for any other type of worship. To highlight the greatness of the reward that awaits those who fast, the Messenger said the following:

---

[19] an-Nasai, Siyam 43.

As for the pleasure of Allah, nothing can deserve more reward than fasting.[20]

Allah will have those who were deprived of food and drinks they desired by fasting eat the fruits of Paradise and drink from the rivers of Paradise.[21]

There is a gate in Paradise called Rayyan (Satiated) through which only the observers of the fast will enter on the Day of Resurrection.[22]

If they who fast earn their sustenance in lawful means, they will not be questioned on the Day of Judgment.[23]

The sleep of those who fast is like worship, and their silence glorifies Allah. The person fasting will be rewarded for their worship and good deeds by the All-Generous Lord. Their prayers are accepted and their sins forgiven.[24]

Fasting will intercede for the believer on the Day of Judgment. The act of fasting will say: "O Allah, I denied them nourishment and marital relations during the day. Let me intercede on their behalf." So, Allah will accept this request and allow fasting to intercede on their behalf.[25]

---

20 an-Nasai, Siyam 43.

21 al-Muttaqi, Ali, Kanz al-Ummal, 3/328.

22 Ibn Maja, Siyam, 1.

23 al-Muttaqi, 3/328.

24 al-Muttaqi, 3/327.

25 al-Munziri, al-Targhib wal-Tarhib, 2/84.

## Why Do Believers Observe the Fast?

Believers observe the fast not because of its spiritual, moral, or material benefits, but rather solely in order to perform perfect and willing obedience to Allah. They submit themselves to the command of Allah merely to seek His pleasure and abstain from things that are otherwise lawful in ordinary life at the behest of Allah. Even if fasting has individual and social benefits, the believer restrains themselves from such desires because the fast has been ordained as a religious duty.

Concerning this issue, Ali ibn Abu Talib states:

> It is the worshipper-merchant who expects something in return for their good deeds. Worship stemming from fear is the deed of a slave. Submitting oneself to the commands of Allah merely in thanks for His blessings is, on the other hand, the worship of a person of freedom.[26]

This most sublime act of worship, as Ali ibn Abu Talib delineates above, is one that is willingly done as a religious duty merely to seek Allah's pleasure. Fasting is one of the prescribed acts of worship that act as training to help the believer achieve this aim.

26 al-Qaari, Ali, Mirqat al-Mafatih, 2/135.

# Chapter 2
# The Merits and Benefits of Fasting

## How does an individual benefit from fasting?

Fasting is one of the five pillars of Islam and it has numerous merits and benefits. However, just as with any other act of worship, Muslims observe fasting not for the benefits, but rather because they wish to totally submit to the pleasure of Allah. The Almighty Allah says in the Qur'an:

وَمَا خَلَقْتُ الْجِنَّ وَالإِنْسَ إِلاَّ لِيَعْبُدُونِ

(which means, "I have not created the jinn and humankind but to know and worship Me alone" [ad-Dhariyat 51:56].)

Therefore, we can see that the main reason why human beings exist is to worship Allah, making worship a fundamental aim in itself. Worship is the ultimate goal of all acts of worship including fasting, prayer, pilgrimage, the prescribed alms, and following His commands regarding what is permitted and what is prohibited.

Believers are aware that worldly benefits are not the ultimate goal of fasting. Muslims draw closer to Allah by abandoning the things they enjoy, and this makes the sincerity of their devotion to Allah all the more evident. They know that Allah will be pleased with them if they abandon worldly comforts for His sake. The reason for their worship is the Divine command and its result is Divine pleasure. As for spiritual merits and anything else that may be gained from performing the fast, these cannot be considered to be the sole results, irrespective of how satisfactory the fruits are. Since believers fast to seek the pleasure of Allah and to gain salvation in the Hereafter, it is clear that the fruits and benefits of the fast are in the Hereafter. Nevertheless, exploring the wisdom behind the act of fasting strengthens the faith of Muslims who are aware that whatever Allah commands is always good and whatever He prohibits is always bad and harmful. This helps them proceed in the awareness that Allah, Who is so compassionate and generous, rewards good deeds both in this world and the Hereafter.

The following sections ask questions and provide answers concerning some of the merits and benefits of fasting; these are not the reasons for observing fasting, but are favors from Allah, the All-Merciful, the All-Compassionate.

## What are the physiological benefits of fasting?

Human beings are created from a body and a soul. A body without a soul is worthless and a soul without a body cannot function in this transient world. Every course of action people take, every bite of food they eat, and every act of worship they observe has a certain effect upon both their body and soul. Abstaining from food helps one reform and renew their physical and spiritual disposition and their behavior. It becomes very difficult for the carnal self to be in harmony with the heart and the spirit if the carnal self acts in whatever way it wishes, eating and drinking whatever and whenever it so desires.

It is universally recognized that there is a close connection between fasting and spiritual insight. Fasting deprives a person of food, drink, and sex during the day, and this denial of physical pleasure is reflected in the spirit, which gains more strength for seeking the pleasure of Allah. Fasting provides the body with a period of physical and psychological rest, giving it the opportunity to cleanse, heal, and rejuvenate itself. This physical detoxification becomes a means for spiritual detoxification. Through fasting, the believer finds it easier to discipline the body in order to elevate the soul and thus approach closer to Allah the Almighty.

The disciplining of one's self by fasting, subduing the physical desires, and keeping vigils in prayer exists in the teachings of Islam. Fasting is a perfect dietary system for the body and ascetic practice for the soul. When frequently observed, the virtues and merits fasting generates are obvious. A person whose only worry is their stomach and who always strives to fill their stomach can be neither healthy nor virtuous, since it is not probable that such a person can conceive of the hunger and misery of other people and will thus not be able to lead a harmonious or healthy life.

## a. Fasting helps the body to rest

Medical authorities are all in agreement that the digestive organs, which begin to function at birth, need an occasional rest. The benefit of fasting during the day for one month is undeniable. When the digestive organs are at a state of rest, the organs of other related systems begin to relax as well. As a result of fasting, the whole body is given a much-desired rest, and an opportunity to renew and rejuvenate. Moreover, the feelings and sentiments of the person fasting are allowed to go beyond the limits of the stomach. They begin to function in harmony with the will of Allah, because they have become pure and refined. Like newly maintained and restored machines in a factory, these emotions begin to serve their real purpose of creation. Bediüzzaman Said Nursi says the following on this issue:

> Many parts of the human body are either in direct or in indirect service of the factory of the stomach. If the factory of the stomach that feeds the carnal self does not cease its activity during the daytime for one month in the year, it keeps these parts busy and focuses their attention on itself, making them temporarily forget their exalted duties peculiar to each. It is because of this, since the earliest times, those closest to Allah have accustomed themselves to austere living with little food and drink to progress in spiritual perfection.
>
> Fasting in Ramadan reminds us that the parts of the body have not been created only for the service of the stomach. In Ramadan, many of those parts take pleasure in lofty spiritual pleasures, instead of material ones. The heart, the spirit, the reason, and the innermost senses of human beings are refined through fasting in that blessed month. Even if the stomach wails during fasting, these senses greatly rejoice.[27]

In order to function well, a machine needs to be maintained and repaired at regular intervals. Otherwise, it will either fall apart or become inefficient. A pupil is allowed to go on holiday after a period of attending classes. An

[27] Nursi, Bediüzzaman Said, Risale-i Nur Külliyatı, Nesil Yayınları, Vol I, "Yirmidokuzuncu Mektub", p. 541.

employee works from morning till evening, and then takes a break in their work and begins to rest. Good, effective performance and the desired output would not be possible if such breaks were not part of the program. The human body is like a factory and its organs are like the machines in the factory. Observing the fast helps the body, which is in fact a factory producing endless energy, thoughts, and feelings, to rest so that it will not breakdown. Fasting also increases the performance of the inner organs in this living factory.

Another important advantage of fasting for the body is that the believer can easily reduce their body weight and thus relax. Today, millions of people suffer from being overweight and spend huge amounts of money trying to lose weight. Although obesity itself is accepted as disease, the most dangerous and harmful aspect is that obesity can result in more harmful diseases, such as hardening of the arteries, high blood pressure, and heart and kidney diseases. Fasting is a remedy for both physical and spiritual ailments.

## b. Fasting protects against diseases

Much has been written about the importance of fasting for both the spirit and the body. A large number of studies have been conducted about the medical benefits and spiritual merits of fasting.

In his book about strengthening the will power, the German professor Gherard advises that all people should observe fasting and states that it is the most effective way to free the soul from the dominance of the body and worldly affairs.[28]

In another study, Dr. Rowy says, "Fasting empowers the endurance of the body against diseases. Today, fasting, which is prescribed in Islam, is being recommended by modern medical institutions as a protective element against ailments." This has been born out in the hospital that is run by Dr. Henri Lehman in Dresden and in clinics directed by Dr. Berscherbenr and Dr. Moliere, where patients undergo a fast as part of their treatment.[29]

In order to underscore the importance of fasting, Muhammad ibn al-Yaman reports: "I asked six questions to six people, but all of them gave the same answer to my six questions. I asked the doctors what the best medicine was. 'Hunger and eating less is the best medicine,' they replied. I asked philosophers what the most effective means of seeking wisdom and truth was and they said, 'It is hunger and eating less.' I asked worshippers what the most useful thing in prostrating oneself before Allah is. They said, 'It is hunger and eating less.' I asked scholars

---

[28] Tabbara, Abdu'l-Fattah, İlmin Işığında İslâmiyet (Islam Under the Light of Sciences), p. 274.

[29] Abdu'r-Razzaq, Nawfal, İslâm ve Modern İlim (Islam and Modern Science), p. 209.

what the best method of collecting knowledge in the mind is and they said, 'It is hunger and eating less.' I asked kings what the best food is. 'It is hunger and eating less,' they said. I asked lovers what the best means of union with one's beloved is and they said, 'It is hunger and eating less.'"

## What is the scientific validity of fasting?

The following article was published in a Pakistani journal, Al-Muslimun. A summary of the study is as follows:

### The Effect of Fasting upon Human Health

*Introduction*

Muslims all over the world observe fasting in the ninth month of the lunar calendar. It is forbidden for Muslims to eat and drink from dawn (that is, approximately one and a half hours before sun-rise) until sunset. But from sunset (iftar) until dawn (sahur), they can eat and drink whatever they want.

Fasting becomes obligatory for every healthy male who has reached the age of 15 or who has reached puberty and for every healthy female who has reached the age of 12 or who has reached puberty. As is stated in the following verse of the Qur'an, fasting is not mandatory for those who are ill or traveling:

وَمَنْ كَانَ مَرِيضًا أَوْ عَلَى سَفَرٍ فَعِدَّةٌ مِنْ أَيَّامٍ أُخَرَ

(which means: "...But if any of you is ill, or on a journey, the prescribed number should be made up from days later..." [al-Baqarah 2:184].)

Because the lunar calendar is eleven days shorter than the solar calendar year, fasting in the month of Ramadan is observed during different months of the Gregorian year. Therefore, Ramadan begins eleven days earlier each year according to the Gregorian calendar.

The fasting hours in the day change in different regions around the world and during different seasons of the year, and therefore the hardship or ease of the fast constantly changes. Sometimes the fast can last for 12 hours and sometimes for 19 hours. Thus, the number of meals may vary from sunset till dawn during different seasons in different countries.

The effects of fasting upon the human body have long been subjected to scientific research. While some studies argue that fasting has certain negative effects, many others have stated that it does not have any detrimental effects upon the organism, as long as it consists only of a change in the eating hours and the daily intake of calories does not change.

### *The Study*

In the research conducted at the Dakar Medical School thirteen volunteers, two of whom were pregnant women, were taken as the experimental group. The main objective was to analyze the effect of fasting upon the human organism. Another object of the same experiment was a 27-year-old woman who was not fasting. Through these studies the effects of fasting upon weight, temperature, pulse, blood pressure of the body, the absorption activities of the cells, and the liquid equilibrium of the organism were analyzed. Blood and urine analyses of the participants were also carried out.

### *Method*

Three of the thirteen participants were women. One of them was 17, another was 27, and the other was 40. The youngest of the male participants was 22 and the oldest was 33. All participants were chosen from middle class and had an intake of 2,500 to 3,000 calories per day. What is more, all of them were healthy people with no known organic or infectious disease.

During the week before Ramadan, the normal values of the participants were recorded in order to compare them later with the values of the observers of fasting during Ramadan. Pre-Ramadan analyses were done before breakfast and during-Ramadan analyses were done after drinking some water, that is, just after breaking the fast with some water (iftar). The analyses were carried out on the first, the tenth, and the last day of Ramadan and once again 30 days after Ramadan.

## *Results*

A general overview of the results is given below. Please see the appendix for further details.

1. Weight Loss or Gain: No significant change in the weight of those who were fasting was observed. Except for two volunteers, the decrease in the weight of those fasting was 2.8 kg at most. The increase in the weight of the pregnant woman was 1.6 kg. Post-Ramadan data show that half of the volunteers regained the weight lost during the month of fasting.

2. Circulatory system: No significant effect of fasting upon pulse or temperature was observed. The hemoglobin rate of the blood was normal. This finding means that the one-month fasting was not a long enough period to cause any degradation in the hemoglobin. In general, no significant change in the blood pressure of the volunteers was evident.

3. Cellular respiration: No significant change in the cellular respiration rate was recorded during Ramadan.

4. The blood sugar rate of the fasters significantly decreased. The decrease rate was 70 mg, which is the lowest rate for the human organism. The rates observed were no higher than 104 mg for any participants.

5. Sugar consumption in the blood: Four of the people fasting, one of whom was a woman, took part in the experiments carried out first before Ramadan and once again on the last day of Ramadan to find out the effect of fast-

ing upon the sugar consumption rate. Analyses demonstrated that there was no significant difference between the glucose rates of fasters and non-fasters. Blood compounds were observed to be stable between the upper and lower normal levels. Moreover, the liver was found to be functioning well.

6. Fluid balance of the body: Most of the people fasting were observed to have a normal fluid balance in their body. Interestingly, some of the people fasting were able to achieve an intake of 2.4 lt. of fluid in twenty-four hours, which is slightly more than what the body requires. Urine discharge (micturation) was normal during the 24-hour period.

General Conclusion: The medical experiments summarized above show clearly that fasting has no negative effects upon the body. Although some changes in the blood sugar values were observed, these were not above physiologically normal levels.

However, it should be made clear that the above-mentioned experiments were carried out on healthy participants. Therefore, the results cannot be extended to those who are sick or handicapped.

## Some Comments

This scientific study conducted at Dakar Medical School has established that fasting is not harmful to the human body. There are many other scientific studies verifying the fact that fasting is even beneficial to the body. Some of its benefits are as follows:

a) The digestive system of the person fasting is able to take a complete rest. The digestive system is an organic mechanism that begins to function with the intake of the first substance that a newborn takes and it continues until the time of death. Therefore, abstaining from food for a few hours is a widely used natural method of providing relief for this system. This method is used before serious operations, as it is recommended for the patient to have an empty stomach before undergoing anesthesia.

b) It is a well-known scientific fact that eating little is more beneficial than eating a lot. That is, so long as the organism attains enough nutrients it is better to eat only at definite hours of the day and to avoid filling the stomach with non-nutritious junk food throughout the day. Actually, fasting brings about this important benefit to the body. The person fasting is advised to eat little, even when breaking the fast. This is a sunnah, or general practice, of the Prophet, and Allah the Almighty says in the Qur'an:

وَمَا آتَاكُمُ الرَّسُولُ فَخُذُوهُ وَمَا نَهَاكُمْ عَنْهُ
فَانْتَهُوا وَاتَّقُوا اللهَ إِنَّ اللهَ شَدِيدُ الْعِقَابِ

(which means: "Whatever the Messenger gives you accept it willingly and whatever he brings you fulfill it, and whatever he forbids you, refrain from it" [al-Hashr 59:7].)

c) It is a well-known fact that over-eating is harmful to the body. Over-eating is among the causes of some common ailments such as heart disease, high blood pressure, and diabetes. Therefore, it is an important curative method to relieve the stomach of one with unhealthy eating habits for one-twelfth of his life. Scientific studies have verified that the ailments mentioned above tend to be less common in regions where fasting is observed as an obligatory practice than in other regions in the world.[30]

## What are the spiritual benefits of fasting?

As was mentioned earlier, every human being has a body and a soul. Both the body and the soul have certain desires and they strive for domination over one another in order to fulfill their desires. Lustful and carnal desires pertain to the body; in connection with this the Holy Qur'an declares:

وَلَقَدْ خَلَقْنَا الإِنْسَانَ مِنْ صَلْصَالٍ مِنْ حَمَإٍ مَسْنُونٍ

(which means: "Verily We created man from potter's clay, from mud molded into shape" [al-Hijr 15:26].)

فَاسْتَفْتِهِمْ أَهُمْ أَشَدُّ خَلْقًا أَمْ مَنْ خَلَقْنَا
إِنَّا خَلَقْنَاهُمْ مِنْ طِينٍ لَازِبٍ

30 Hawwa, Sa'id, Islam, pp. 170-176.

(which means: "Just ask their opinion: Are they the more difficult to create, or those (angels, the Heavens, and the Earth) whom We have created. Surely We have created you from sticky clay" [as-Saffat 37:11].)

خَلَقَ الإِنْسَانَ مِنْ صَلْصَالٍ كَالْفَخَّارِ

(which means: "He created humankind from dry clay like earthen vessels" [ar-Rahman 55:14].)

The other aspect of human beings is the soul, which is a reminder of the wisdom in the creation of humanity and which guides them toward good deeds, helping them to contemplate and admire the spiritual worlds. The soul rejoices and relishes in great pleasures even when the body is crying out for a sip of water or a morsel of food. Fasting helps human beings to understand the dark and heinous nature of certain deeds and avoid them.

When the dominance of the soul over the body weakens or when the body becomes dominant, then human beings become slaves to their carnal desires. They pay no heed to the intellect or to religious admonitions and spend all their energy trying to quench thirst and hunger for worldly delights. Their only concern is to find new ways of satisfying their carnal desires. They have to invent substances that increase the appetite, that aid digestion, or even act as stimulants. "Such people are like a donkey or an ox even if they are at the peak of science, culture, and civilization. They will commute between the dining room and the toilet all their life and will have no time for any principles or for the eternal life. All their faculties will die, except for those pertaining to lust, food, drink, and foolish entertainment."[31] No depiction can be more precise or more elegant than that of the Qur'an:

وَالَّذِينَ كَفَرُوا يَتَمَتَّعُونَ وَيَأْكُلُونَ كَمَا
تَأْكُلُ الأَنْعَامُ وَالنَّارُ مَثْوًى لَهُمْ

(which means: "...as for those who disbelieve, they shall enjoy this world and eat as cattle eat; and the Fire shall be their abode" [Muhammad 47:12].)

## a. Fasting helps the believer to remember Allah

Every hour, even every second of the daily life of a person who fasts leads to the remembrance of Allah, reunion with the Almighty, and the blessings He has bestowed upon human beings. Fasting brings about this remembrance in two ways: It makes the believers long for eternal blessings by showing them that the worldly favors are transient. The pleasure that the believers who fast enjoy when they break their fast and thus end a form of suffering also makes them remember Allah and the eternal blessings He has created for them in the Hereafter. Although those who suffer from hunger and thirst from dawn until sunset apparently feel pain, the favors that await them in the other world soothe their sufferings.

[31] Al-Nadwi, pp. 194, 195.

Moreover, they find pleasure in contemplating reunion with the Almighty Allah; it is for Him that believers abstain from food, drink, and other corporeal desires. The Noble Messenger, peace and blessings be upon him, says: "There are two pleasures for the fasting person, one at the time of breaking their fast, and the other at the time when they will meet their Lord."[32]

## b. Fasting helps the believer ascend to the level of the angels

Human beings have characteristics and faculties that are both carnal and spiritual. When they avoid their carnal feelings, these feelings weaken and the spiritual faculties prosper. Allah the Almighty has provided humanity with the will power to descend from a most exalted rank to the lowest of the low, or vice versa. Therefore, sometimes humans can be more revered than the angels and become closer to their Lord, while at other times some people are worse than any devil.

لَقَدْ خَلَقْنَا الإِنْسَانَ فِي أَحْسَنِ تَقْوِيمٍ ❁ ثُمَّ رَدَدْنَاهُ
أَسْفَلَ سَافِلِينَ ❁ إِلَّا الَّذِينَ آمَنُوا وَعَمِلُوا
الصَّالِحَاتِ فَلَهُمْ أَجْرٌ غَيْرُ مَمْنُونٍ

[32] al-Bukhari, Tawhid, 35; Muslim, Siyam, 164; at-Tirmidhi, Siyam, 55; an-Nasai, Siyam, 41; Ibn Maja, Siyam, 1; Ibn Hanbal, 1/446; ad-Darimi, Sawm, 50.

(which means: "Surely We have created human of the best stature as the perfect pattern of creation; then We have reduced him to the lowest of the low. Except those who believe and do good, righteous deeds, so there is for them a reward constant and beyond measure" [at-Tin 95:4–6].)

The difference between human beings and angels is that humans have a carnal soul. Angels cannot eat, drink, have sexual relations, or be rebellious to their Lord. Because of their intrinsic characteristics they are occupied with the remembrance of Allah (dhikr) and worship continuously:

يَعْلَمُ مَا بَيْنَ أَيْدِيهِمْ وَمَا ❁ لاَ يَسْبِقُونَهُ بِالْقَوْلِ وَهُمْ بِأَمْرِهِ يَعْمَلُونَ
خَلْفَهُمْ وَلاَ يَشْفَعُونَ إِلاَّ لِمَنِ ارْتَضَى وَهُمْ مِنْ خَشْيَتِهِ مُشْفِقُونَ

(which means: "They speak not before He speaks, and they act in all things by His Command. He knows what is before them and what is behind them, and they do not intercede except for him whom He approves and for fear of Him they tremble" [al-Anbiya' 21:27–8].)

As for humans, they need food and drink to maintain their physical existence. They can rebel and they can commit sins. However, a true believer who observes fasting, controlling their desires and abstaining from food, drink, sexual intercourse, backbiting, and brutality is able to achieve an angelic stance. Such people may even surpass the angels. Allah is pleased with them and He holds them up to the angels as an example.[33]

## c. Fasting teaches the worth of blessings

Allah the Almighty has ornamented the Earth with numerous blessings and has given them all to humanity, the caliphs, or vicegerents, of Allah on Earth. Each day they receive lavishly prepared dining tables, one after another. Their sustenance is sent to them from the Heavens via the trees, each of which gives a different fruit in a different season of the year and the Earth nourishes them with every kind of delicious provisions.

وَآتَاكُمْ مِنْ كُلِّ مَا سَأَلْتُمُوهُ وَإِنْ تَعُدُّوا نِعْمَةَ
اللهِ لاَ تُحْصُوهَا إِنَّ الإِنْسَانَ لَظَلُومٌ كَفَّارٌ

(which means: "He has granted you all that you would ask of Him. Should you attempt to count Allah's blessings, you cannot calculate them. But humankind is innately inclined to extreme misjudgment and ingratitude" [Ibrahim 14:34].)

Both the Earth and the skies were created to serve humanity. Allah, the most Gracious, gave us countless favors but unfortunately, for the most part we are unaware

33 Munziri, al-Targhib wal-Tarhib, 2/99.

of these bounties. We are like a fish that is in the sea but is unaware of the water. Fasting helps us to become aware of the blessings of Allah and to appreciate them.

### d. Fasting teaches a person how to economize

Fasting teaches people how to economize, a form of behavior that is recommended in Islam. During Ramadan, fasting takes on the role of a teacher who instructs us on how to economize. People who are accustomed to buying whatever they want without thinking too much will learn to be thrifty and careful. No matter how thirsty or hungry they are, they have to wait until sunset before eating or drinking something. The pleasure the believer obtains at the time of breaking the fast becomes greater than the pleasure the glutton obtains from overeating, as this is accompanied by a weariness and lack of appetite resulting from such excesses. Through fasting believers are taught to economize, and their frugality leads to contentment.

### e. Fasting exalts the soul

The body, as well as the soul, has some needs and desires. The physical body of a human is comparatively small, but the soul is infinite. The countless tendencies, desires, feelings, dreams, thoughts, and ideas of humanity are like an index of the universe.

Therefore, nothing but worship, the greatest and the most sublime way of reaching Allah, can advance and improve the soul and faculties of such a being, fulfill their tendencies and desires, broaden and arrange their ideas, control their powers pertaining to lust and anger, allow them to reach their preordained perfection and bind them to Allah the Almigthy. Fasting, which is an act of worship, comprises all these characteristics. The Messenger of Allah says: "There are alms for everything. Observing the fast is the alms for the body and observing the fast is half of patience."[34] Daily Prayer is the main pillar of religion, fasting is the main pillar of the soul, while the prescribed alms is the main pillar of the community. That is, a religion without Daily Prayers, a soul that does not fast, and a community that does not contribute to charity cannot stand upright. In the same way that food nourishes the body, fasting nourishes the soul. It is as difficult to lead a religious life without fasting as it is to live without eating.

Therefore, although it changes in form and duration, fasting has been accepted as an important fundamental of all religions; the main aim of religious fasting is to purify the soul. Moreover, Prophets, who are guides for the purification and perfection of the soul, observed fasting during the preparation phase of their difficult missions. While fasting and worshipping during the month of Ramadan in the Hira cave on top of a mountain in soli-

[34] at-Tirmidhi, Daawat, 86; Ibn Maja, Siyam, 44.

tude, Prophet Muhammad, peace and blessings be upon him, was called to Prophethood at the age of forty. The Bible mentions that Jesus fasted for forty days in the desert before starting his ministry. Similarly, Moses received the Ten Commandments after fasting for forty days. This is another proof of the fact that fasting is an influential factor in the maturation and purification of human beings.

To conclude, the soul is purified and refined through fasting. Those who want to improve their spiritual faculties should observe the fast. In other words, those who do not fast become captives of their body and cannot renew and excel their soul.

## f. Fasting controls worldly desires

People need to restrain the endless desires of their carnal soul, for the desires and habits of the carnal soul are like lethal poison or forces that push them to degrade themselves. The carnal soul continuously commands human beings to commit sins. According to a Qur'anic decree Prophet Joseph describes the carnal soul in the most eloquent way:

وَمَا أُبَرِّئُ نَفْسِي إِنَّ النَّفْسَ لَأَمَّارَةٌ بِالسُّوءِ إِلاَّ
مَا رَحِمَ رَبِّي إِنَّ رَبِّي غَفُورٌ رَحِيمٌ

(which means: "Nor do I absolve my own self of blame: the human soul is certainly prone to evil, unless my

Lord does bestow His Mercy: but surely my Lord is All-Forgiving, Most Merciful" [Yusuf 12:53].)

It is very difficult to satisfy the carnal soul; the more you give the more it demands. the Noble Messenger used to supplicate: "O Allah, I seek refuge in You from incapacity, from sloth, from cowardice, from miserliness, decrepitude and from the torment of the grave. O Allah, grant to my soul a sense of righteousness and purify it, for You are the Best Purifier. You are the soul's Protecting Friend and Guardian. O Allah, I seek refuge in You from the knowledge which does not benefit, from the heart that does not have the fear of Allah, from the soul that does not feel contented and the supplication that is not responded."[35] In another tradition he seeks refuge in Allah from evils, troubles, and atrocities of the soul.[36]

Fasting is also like armor against fornication, a sin that endangers family life. The Noble Messenger advises those who do not have the economic means to marry to observe the fast in order to avoid sins.

Actually, fasting is an effective means of taking the carnal soul under control. Therefore, fasting, which is obligatory in many religions and accepted as a practical means demonstrating one's fear of and respect for Allah

---

[35] Muslim, Dhikr 73.

[36] at-Tirmidhi, Daawat, 14.

(taqwa), was established as one of the pillars of Islam. Allah says in the Qur'an:

يَا أَيُّهَا الَّذِينَ آمَنُوا كُتِبَ عَلَيْكُمُ الصِّيَامُ كَمَا كُتِبَ
عَلَى الَّذِينَ مِنْ قَبْلِكُمْ لَعَلَّكُمْ تَتَّقُونَ

(which means: "O you who believe! Prescribed for you is the Fast, as it was prescribed for those before you, so that you may deserve Allah's protection against the temptations of your carnal soul and attain piety" [al-Baqarah 2:183].)

Fasting is the reins and bit that restrain the carnal self. It hinders human beings from becoming pharaohs. It is reported that the Prophet said: "Allah inflicted certain sort of punishments upon the carnal self. First He put the carnal self in the fire and asked: 'Who are you, who am I?' The carnal self said: 'You are you, I am me.' Then Allah restrained the self with hunger and asked again: 'Who are you, who am I?' The final answer of the self was: 'You are the Owner of the worlds and I am one of Your humble servants.'"

Finally, human beings can prevent their souls from being rebellious to the Almighty Allah and train them to become an obedient servant by fasting. People who observe the fast become aware that during the fast their soul is as pure as that of the angels. When fasting they are able to understand that they cannot do anything unless they are so permitted, that they cannot have even a sip of water without the permission of Allah and thus they perceive that they are not the owner but rather the owned and they are not the master but the servant. In the end, they become aware of their endless weakness, destitution, and deficiencies, and thus prepare to knock at the door of the All-Merciful and the All-Compassionate in a grateful manner.

## g. Fasting protects a person against sins

Committing sins is a kind of inner depression, perversion, and contradiction of the natural disposition. The sinners are wretched and miserable and they submit all their faculties and talents to Satan and thus expose themselves to the pangs of conscience. If they go on committing sins, then they will lose control over their body and soul and will be able neither to resist Satan nor to renew themselves.

There are thousands of different kinds of sins in everyday life. They are like snakes that wait for a chance to strike. It is very difficult to avoid sin in a world full of evil. Only will power, if it is as strong as steel, can help to resist Satan and protect one's purity. Otherwise, it is easy to predict that a person will stray off the right path and end up in a pit of fire.

In fact, fasting is a precaution and a guarantee against such a threat. For some people it is a shelter against deviation. It is warning against Satan and all kinds of evil. It protects the person fasting like armor and becomes a gateway to Paradise on the Day of Judgment and a blessed friend who offers bowls of water from Kawthar—the sacred fountain in Paradise. The Noble Messenger, peace and blessings be upon him, recommended that young people who cannot afford to get married fast in order to diminish their sexual desire and thus refrain from engaging in illegal sexual relations.

Fasting is a training that enables the believer to resist the carnal desires. A person who is trained through fasting can suppress their fleshly desires not only when fasting, but also when they are not observing the fast. Fasting is far more than being hungry; it is also a form of training for the various elements of body, such as the emotions, senses, eyes, ears, and heart. These aspects of the human body observe fasting as well, and thus they are trained to avoid blasphemy. Allah's pleasure and consent becomes the pivot of the whole life of the believer; a person who fasts does so with all the parts of their body and with all their senses. Surely, a person who is fasting in this manner will be given a most rewarding life in Paradise. Here is evidence from the Prophet's tradition: "Whoever can guarantee the chastity of what is between their two jaw-bones and what is between their two legs (i.e. the tongue and the private parts), I guarantee Paradise for them."[37]

[37] al-Bukhari, Riqaq, 23

The most effective way of protecting the chastity of the tongue is to observe fasting. All the organs of the body work energetically when the stomach is full. Therefore, the strength of fleshly desires is at its peak and at such a time it is difficult to refrain the tongue from blasphemous talk and backbiting, which are threats for the eternal life. The only way of taking the tongue under control is to reduce the strength of the desires of the carnal self and the only way of doing this is to observe fasting. Abstinence is emphasized in a tradition as: "If one of you is fasting, they should avoid sexual relations with their spouse and quarreling, and if somebody should fight or quarrel with them, they should say, 'I am fasting,'"[38] "Whoever does not give up forged speech and evil actions, Allah is not in need of their leaving their food and drink (i.e. Allah will not accept their fast)."[39]

To conclude, the best fast is that which is observed by various parts of body in addition to the stomach, such as the eyes, ears, heart, mind, and intellect. That is, fasting is observed best when sins and profanities are avoided and when the stomach, the biggest factory inside the human body, is taken under control and thus decreases the strength of the other faculties; this is the best way to reach this goal.[40]

---

[38] al-Bukhari, Sawm, 9; an-Nasai, Siyam, 42; Ibn Hanbal, 2/273

[39] al-Bukhari, Sawm, 8

[40] Nursi, Vol I, Mektubat, p. 540

## h. Fasting teaches how to be trustworthy

Fasting teaches believers to be trustworthy and to protect everything that is entrusted to them. Those who fast know well that Allah knows what is in their minds, and that He is the Knower of the Unseen (Ghayb), all that lies beyond sense and perception and are thus hidden to our perception. Nobody but Allah knows whether they are observing the fast or not. A person abstains from food, drink and all kinds of sins only for Allah. They refrain from eating when they can and even if there is no one to see them. They go on fasting when it is possible to do otherwise. They do not break the fast because they do not want to breach Allah's trust in them. This conduct is reflected in every action of Muslims who observe fasting and therefore they are cautious and careful in protecting all goods that are consigned to them, in awareness that the All-Knowing Allah sees and knows whatever they do.

## i. Fasting teaches how to keep oaths and promises

Fasting, in which trustworthiness is best characterized, is the best act of worship, as it is a kind of agreement between Allah and His servants. The believing servants will desist from certain things for a definite period of time and thus show that they are loyal to their oaths. Moreover, by doing this, they will improve their sense of loyalty and trustworthiness through fasting and this characteristic will become a part of their lives. They will become the epitome of trustworthiness in social life and this attribute will make them happier in both worlds.

## j. Fasting teaches contentment

Fasting becomes a barrier between people who are fasting and the evil delusions that Satan continuously whisper into their ears. It gives the believers the strength to deny the carnal self and Satan control over the body, for the believer's faculties are closed to physical nourishment, sensual relations, and worldly affairs. Thus, they free themselves of the pressures of their carnal self and body and begin to lead a life of honor and dignity. This is the characteristic consigned to believers by the Almighty Allah. In the Noble Qur'an Allah says:

وَلِلّٰهِ الْعِزَّةُ وَلِرَسُولِهِ وَلِلْمُؤْمِنِينَ

(which means "...to Allah belong all honor and might, and thus to His Messenger and the believers..." [al-Munafiqun 63:8].)

## k. Fasting teaches patience

One of the major benefits of fasting is that it trains believers to be patient. While observing the fast, believers undergo a period of training, because they do not eat when they feel hunger, do not drink when they feel thirst, and patiently say, "I am fasting," when somebody upsets them. When they thus bind their hands, feet, tongue, lips, and ears, patience becomes Buraq,[41] a heavenly steed, taking them on their journey toward the Almighty Allah and His pleasure.

The nervous system plays a very important role in the body. If the nerves belonging to the tongue are paralyzed then a person cannot speak. If the nerves belonging to the legs are paralyzed a person cannot walk. Our life is endangered if the nerves do not work properly. Nervousness is a state of mind related to the nerves and the nervous system. A person who is nervous is uneasy and finds it hard to be patient. Many fights and quarrels occur when people are feeling nervous and suffer from the resulting impatience. In a tradition, the Prophet says: "Fasting is one half of patience, patience, too, is one half of faith."[42] Thus, it is evident that fasting is related to faith. People whose faith is strong do not commit crimes or sins; they can control their nerves and they are patient. It is easier for those who observe fasting to be patient, for fasting dissuades the unlawful desires that mislead the soul.

## I. Fasting teaches perseverance and endurance

People may lose everything they have: their wealth, their friends and even their children. They may become poor and miserable any time, any place. They may become afflicted by incessant sorrows all at one time. Therefore,

41 Buraq is the name of the heavenly mount, the nature of which is not known, which Allah's Messenger rode on the night of Ascension.

42 Ibn Maja, Siyam, 44

they need to prepare their body and soul for such unexpected misfortunes.

Observers of the fast are equipped and prepared for such calamities because they are able to show patience against the most basic sources of distress, such as hunger and thirst and to adjust their bodies and souls to more sorrowful events and situations that they may have to face in the future. In the case of such an affliction, they will not easily lose heart or give up struggling for better conditions. They will persevere and fight against problems, difficulties, and torments.

What is more, fasting re-molds and re-shapes the souls of the observers of the fast and grants them a strong, resolute, and unyielding character. Those who fast do not give way to worldly pains and do not yield to injustice. Thus, fasting trains believers so that they never give up their principles for any worldly gain. This is the perfect and ideal character defined and praised in Islam.

### m. Fasting brings about a sense of order and harmony

Fasting provides the believer with a sense of order and harmony. Such time periods of fasting as sahur (pre-dawn meal) and iftar (breaking the fast in the evening) help the believer toward a more orderly and harmonious life. Believers are more eager to observe the Daily Prayers at the pre-determined time for each Prayer. Also, they observe the congregational Tarawih Prayer, which only occurs in Ramadan, the month of fasting. All these time periods bring discipline and harmony to the life of believers.

## What are the benefits of fasting for the society?

### a. Fasting ensures the unity and harmony of society

Fasting (especially when observed in Ramadan) leads to a positive change in the attitudes of the believers towards each other. The sense of empathy it invokes helps the faster understand other people better and makes it easier for them to make friends and socialize. The usual activities of Ramadan that are common to all believers, such as fasting during the same month, waiting for the time to break the fast in the evening, congregational Tarawih Prayers observed in the mosque after breaking the fast, and getting up at night to have the pre-dawn meal (sahur) before beginning the fast all foster the brotherhood and affection among the believers. In particular, the Night of Power (Laylat al-Qadr) and the Eid celebration (Eid al-Fitr) at the end of Ramadan strengthen the social ties among believers. Allah's Messenger says: "The similitude of believers in regard to mutual love, affection, and fellow-feeling is that of one body; when any limb aches, the whole body aches because of sleeplessness and fever."[43] Therefore, believers feel themselves to be the limbs of one body and this feeling strengthens the solidarity and friendship in the community.

Actually, during Ramadan all members of a family sit at the table and wait together for the time to break the fast; in Islam it is recommended that all family members sit at the dining table together. Inviting relatives, friends, neighbors and even strangers to iftar (the meal that one eats to break the fast) is highly recommended as well. Friends converse and wait together for the same event, and experience the same feelings. They feel tenderhearted toward each other, and in fact toward all living beings, because of the hunger they feel. They have neither time nor energy for enmity or grudges. These affectionate feelings continue after Ramadan, for fasting is a period of training.

### b. Fasting raises awareness of the situation of the poor

Fasting teaches the rich, who eat good, nutritious food and never suffer from hunger, what hunger is. When they stay hungry and thirsty for a period they begin to think about the poor and feel empathy for them. The rich then desire to help the poor and needy, as fasting makes it

[43] al-Bukhari, Adab, 27; Muslim, Birr, 66; Ibn Hanbal, Musnad, 4/270.

possible for them to empathize with the poor and to see the hard and challenging conditions they live in. On the other hand, because of the kindness and compassion of the rich, the poor are less likely to feel envy and hatred toward those who are better off. Thus, a change of attitude on both sides can occur. The enmity between both social strata can be brought to an end in this way with peace and security prevailing in society.

The idea of restoring social justice, security, and peace so easily is quite exciting as well as being difficult to believe. However, this is a fact based on experience and on the teachings of Islam. The Messenger of Allah says: "Those who are full while their neighbors are hungry are not of us."[44]

It is clear that there is deep wisdom in obeying the rules prescribed by Allah and carrying out such acts of worship that have many personal and social benefits, even if only some of these benefits have been made known to us. Abstaining from food not only makes us healthy, but also makes us a perfect member of the community.

### c. Fasting develops dignity

People who have persevered against hardships, such as hunger and thirst, and have thus trained their body and soul, can challenge and overcome every difficulty they may encounter in life. Hunger and thirst cease to be great

44 Ibn Hanbal, Musnad, 1/55.

threats for such people. Hunger pains are no longer a chain that holds them back. Such people can protect their self-respect and dignity at any cost. They will not beg for money or food, even when they are hungry.

Yogis can go on living without food or drink for six months, even though they are not seeking the pleasure of Allah, therefore it is not hard to understand how believers feel secure that with the help and consent of their Lord they can easily endure more physical suffering without degrading themselves before other people if they fall on hard times. But those who have never fasted and thus immunized their body against hunger will most probably abase themselves and begin to beg for food in order to satisfy their hunger when they find themselves having to do without.

# Chapter 3
# Types of Fasts

## What are the various types of fasts?

### Types of Fasts

1. Obligatory Fasts
2. Supererogatory Fasts
3. Forbidden Fasts

## What are the types of obligatory (*fard*) fasts?

### a. Fasting in the month of Ramadan

Fasting is one of the obligations that must be fulfilled by every Muslim. The obligation of fasting is mandatory on a person who is a Muslim, is sane, has reached puberty, is healthy, and who is not on a journey; for women, they must not be menstruating, pregnant, or nursing (with the last two conditions, fasting is not obligatory if the health of the mother or the baby will be affected by the fast.) People who have fulfilled these prerequisites must observe fasting in the month of Ramadan (the 9th month of the lunar calendar) as described by the Noble Prophet and the Holy Qur'an.

## b. Making up for missed fasts

A Muslim must make up for any obligatory fasts that they have missed. That is, if they were ill during Ramadan, or traveling, or in the case of women, if they were menstruating, pregnant, or nursing, the days that they missed must be made up at a later date. These fasts can be observed at any time from the end of Ramadan of one year until the beginning of the following Ramadan. This obligation is decreed in the Qur'an:

وَمَنْ كَانَ مَرِيضًا أَوْ عَلَى سَفَرٍ فَعِدَّةٌ مِنْ أَيَّامٍ أُخَرَ

(which means: "The fast is for a fixed number of days. If any of you be so ill that he cannot fast or is on a journey, then he must fast the same number of days on other days..." [al-Baqarah 2:185].)

Any supererogatory fasts must also be redeemed if one breaks this non-obligatory fast before the iftar time. If acts of non-obligatory worship, such as supererogatory Prayers and fasting, are interrupted before their completion, they must be made up later. Mother Aisha, may Allah be pleased with her, related: "Some food was presented to me and Hafsah. We were fasting, but broke our fast. Then the Messenger of Allah entered upon us. We said to him: 'A gift was presented to us; we coveted it and we broke our fast.' The Messenger of Allah said: 'There is no harm to you; keep a fast another day to make it up.'"[45]

## c. Fasts in fulfillment of vows (*nadhir*)

The word nadhir means promising to do something to attain the pleasure of Allah and thus putting oneself under an obligation. In Islam, it is a highly valued practice to fulfill a promised act that is accepted as worship only to seek Allah's pleasure and forgiveness. A believer can say: "I promise to fast tomorrow for Allah's pleasure." To give another example, a believer might make a promise to help the poor. Then it becomes obligatory on the believer to fulfill the promised deed as Allah has said (as translated): "Let them… fulfill their vows" (al-Hajj 22:29). The Noble Prophet said: "Whoever makes a vow to submit to Allah, must submit; whoever makes a vow to rebel against Allah, must not rebel."[46]

## d. Fasts of expiation for religious offenses (*kaffara*)

Neglecting the fast of Ramadan willingly, on purpose, or without any acceptable reason is an unpardonable sin.

[45] Abu Dawud, Siyam, 73; at-Tirmidhi, Sawm, 36; Ibn Hanbal, 6/263.
[46] an-Nasai, Iman, 41.

Because of the countless virtues and merits of fasting during the month of Ramadan, even a perpetual fast at other times of the year will not compensate for missing one day of fasting neglected in Ramadan. However, in order to expiate for reckless and deliberate break of a fasting day in Ramadan, the believer must fast for two successive months. This is stated in the following tradition of the Messenger reported by Abu Hurayra: "While we were sitting with the Messenger of Allah a man came and said, 'O Messenger of Allah! I have been ruined.' The Prophet asked him what the matter was. He replied, 'I had sexual intercourse with my wife while I was fasting.' The Prophet asked him, 'Can you afford to free a slave?' He replied in the negative. The Prophet asked him, 'Can you fast for two successive months?' He replied in the negative. The Prophet asked him, 'Can you afford to feed sixty poor persons?' He replied in the negative. The Prophet kept silent and while we were in that state, a big basket full of dates was brought to the Prophet. He asked, 'Where is the questioner?' He replied, 'I (am here).' The Messenger of Allah said to him, 'Take this (basket of dates) and give it in charity.' The man said, 'Should I give it to a person poorer than I? By Allah, there is no family between its (i.e. Madina's) two mountains who is poorer than I.' The Prophet smiled and then said, 'Feed your family with it.'"[47]

---

[47] al-Bukhari, Sawm, 30; Muslim, Siyam, 81; at-Tirmidhi, Sawm, 28.

To sum up, expiation is required if one has marital relations, eats, or drinks intentionally during the fast of Ramadan. The expiation consists of freeing a slave, or if not possible, then fasting for two successive months. If this is not possible, then the expiation is to feed sixty needy people.

## What are the types of supererogatory fasts?

This kind of fast is an act of voluntary (nawafil) worship that is observed to draw closer to Allah. In order to stress the importance of supererogatory fasts, in a hadith qudsi (the meaning of which was revealed, but was put into words by the Prophet) he says: "...the most beloved things with which My servant comes nearer to Me is what I have enjoined upon him; and My servant continues to come closer to Me by performing voluntary worship until I love him, and I become his sense of hearing with which he hears, and his sense of sight with which he sees, and his hand with which he grips, and his leg with which he walks..."[48]

In another tradition, the Noble Prophet relates the virtues of voluntary worship as follows: "Anyone who fasts for one day for Allah's pleasure, Allah will keep their face away from the Hell for the distance that is covered by a journey of seventy years."[49]

---

[48] al-Bukhari, Riqaq, 38; Ibn Hanbal, Musnad, 4/256.

[49] al-Bukhari, Jihad, 36; Muslim, Siyam, 167; Ibn Maja, Siyam, 34; an-Nasai, Siyam, 44.

## a. The fast of Prophet David

The Noble Prophet said that the second most virtuous fast after the obligatory fast is that of Prophet David, peace be upon him. Abdullah ibn Amr relates: "The Messenger of Allah was informed that I had said: 'By Allah, I will fast all the days and pray all the nights as long as I live.' On hearing this, the Prophet asked me if this was true. I told him that this was so. He said, 'You cannot do that. So, sometimes fast and sometimes do not fast. Pray and sleep. Fast for three days a month, for the reward of a good deed is multiplied by ten times, and thus the fasting of three days every month equals the fasting of a year.' I said, 'O Messenger of Allah! I can do more than that.' He said, 'Fast every third day.' I said: 'I can do more than that.' He said: 'Fast on alternate days; this is the fasting of David, which is the most virtuous supererogatory fast.' I said, 'O Messenger of Allah! I can do more than that.' He said, 'There is nothing better than that.'"[50]

In another tradition Allah's Messenger says: "The fasting of Prophet David is the most virtuous voluntary fast. He used to fast one day and break his fast the next day."[51]

---

50 al-Bukhari, Anbiya, 37; Muslim Siyam, 181; Abu Dawud, Sawm, 53; an-Nasai, Siyam, 86.

51 al-Bukhari, Sawm, 56; Muslim, Siyam, 189; Abu Dawud, Siyam, 76.

## b. Fasting on Mondays and Thursdays

The Messenger of Allah, peace and blessings be upon him, used to fast two days a week, namely on Mondays and Thursdays, and he rarely missed these two days. Mother Aisha, may Allah be pleased with her, said, "The Messenger of Allah used to give extra care to fasting on Mondays and Thursdays."[52] The reason for singling out Mondays and Thursdays is the fact that it is on these two days, as explained in a tradition, that the deeds are raised into the Heavens and these are the days of forgiveness. Usama ibn Zayd related: "Upon seeing that the Messenger of Allah observed fasting on Mondays and Thursdays I asked him why. He said: 'The deeds of humanity are exhibited to Allah the Almighty every Monday and Thursday. I want to be fasting when my deeds are exhibited to Allah.'"[53]

According to another report, our beloved Prophet was asked about fasting on Mondays, whereupon he said: "It was the day on which I was born, it was the day on which I was commissioned with (the mission of) Prophethood and the Divine Revelation was sent to me."[54]

---

52 at-Tirmidhi, Sawm, 44; an-Nasai, Siyam, 36; Ibn Maja, Siyam, 42; Ibn Hanbal 6/80.

53 at-Tirmidhi, Sawm, 44; an-Nasai, Siyam, 70.

54 Muslim, Siyam, 197.

## c. Fasting on three days every month

Fasting on three days of each month is one of the traditions of Allah's Messenger. Fasting on the 13th, 14th, and 15th days of the lunar month is believed to be more virtuous. The reward for fasting on these days is equal to fasting the whole year, as the reward for one good deed is multiplied by ten. Allah says in the Holy Qur'an:

مَنْ جَاءَ بِالْحَسَنَةِ فَلَهُ عَشْرُ أَمْثَالِهَا وَمَنْ جَاءَ بِالسَّيِّئَةِ فَلاَ يُجْزَى إِلاَّ مِثْلَهَا وَهُمْ لاَ يُظْلَمُونَ

(which means: "Whoever comes to Allah with a good deed will have ten times as much, and whoever comes with an evil deed will be recompensed with only the like of it; and they will not be wronged" [al-An'am 6:160].)

So if we multiply the three days of fasting each month by ten, this makes thirty. That is, someone who fasts on three days each month is rewarded as if he has fasted the whole year. Abu Hurayra reported that the Prophet advised him to observe these three things: (1) to fast three days a month; (2) to pray two cycles (rakats) of Duha Prayer (a supererogatory Prayer that is prayed before noon); and (3) to pray Witr Prayer before sleeping.[55] In another report by Abu Dharr, Allah's Messenger said, "O Abu Dharr!

[55] al-Bukhari, Sawm, 60; an-Nasai, Siyam, 81.

When you fast three days of the month, fast on the 13th, 14th and 15th days.[56]

## d. Fasting on the Day of Arafat

Believers that are not performing the Hajj can fast on the day of Arafat. The day of Arafat is the ninth day of the lunar month of Dhu'l-Hijja. The Prophet said, "Fasting on the day of Arafat absolves the sins of two years: the previous year and the coming year."[57] To underline the virtue of this day he also said, "There is no day when Allah sets free more servants from Hell than the Day of Arafat."[58] It is forbidden for people that are performing the Hajj to fast on the day of Arafat. This is a mercy for pilgrims because fasting would exert more hardships on them, and they would not be able to perform the rituals of Hajj well.

## e. Fasting six days of Shawwal

The month of Shawwal follows Ramadan in the lunar calendar. It is a tradition of our beloved Prophet to fast six days in Shawwal, for he said: "Whoever observes the fast

56 an-Nasai, Siyam, 84; Ibn Hanbal, 5/152.

57 Muslim, Siyam, 196.

58 Muslim, Hajj, 436.

of Ramadan and follows it with six days of fast in Shawwal, it is as if he has fasted the whole year."[59]

A man who fasts on six days of Shawwal is rewarded as if he fasted the whole year. Because it is decreed in the Qur'an that whoever performs a good act will receive ten times its like.[60] Fasting in the month of Ramadan equals ten months, and six fasting days in Shawwal is equal to two months. Thus, fasting six days in Shawwal together with Ramadan fast is equal to fasting the whole year.

It is better to observe voluntary or redeeming fasts on Mondays and Thursdays in Shawwal, for good deeds are presented to Allah on Mondays and Thursdays. The Prophet said, "Deeds are presented to Allah on Monday and Thursday and I would like my deeds to be presented while I am fasting."[61]

## f. Fasting on the Day of Ashura

According to Abdullah ibn Abbas, when Prophet Muhammad, peace and blessings be upon him, came to Madina, he saw the Jews fasting on the tenth of the month of Muharram in celebration of Prophet Moses' victory over the Pharaoh. Upon this, our beloved Prophet fasted on

---

[59] Muslim, Siyam, 204; at-Tirmidhi, Sawm, 52; Ibn Maja, Siyam, 33.

[60] See al-An'am 6:160.

[61] at-Tirmidhi, Sawm, 44; an-Nasai, Siyam, 70.

Ashura day and ordered the Companions to fast as well.[62] This practice was followed until the fast of Ramadan became obligatory. Then, the Prophet let the believers decide for themselves whether to fast on the day of Ashura or not. He said, "It is without a doubt that the Day of Ashura is one of Allah's days. From now on, who so wishes should fast on that day; who so wishes does not have to."[63]

## g. Fasting in the month of Sha'ban

Fasting in the month of Sha'ban was one of the fasts observed by the Noble Prophet. He was keen to fast in this month, which is the eighth month of the lunar year and precedes Ramadan. There are reports that the Prophet used to fast most of this month or all of the month, joining it with Ramadan. Mother Umm Salama, may Allah be pleased with her, narrated that she never saw the Messenger of Allah fasting for a whole month except for Sha'ban, which he combined with Ramadan.[64] Mother Aisha says, "I never saw the Prophet of Allah fast for a whole month except the month of Ramadan, and did not see him fasting in any month more than in the month of Sha'ban."[65]

---

[62] al-Bukhari, Sawm, 69; Muslim, Siyam, 127; Abu Dawud, Sawm, 63.

[63] al-Bukhari, Sawm, 69; Muslim, Siyam, 116; Muwatta, Siyam, 34.

[64] Abu Dawud, Sawm, 57.

[65] al-Bukhari, Sawm, 52; Muslim, Siyam, 176; Abu Dawud, Sawm, 59.

## What are the forbidden fasts?

### a. Continuous fasting

A continuous fast, which is called wisaal in Islamic terminology, is the practice of fasting for two or more successive days without a break. The Prophet, the most merciful and compassionate of human beings, warned those who followed this practice and advised them not to observe this kind of fast. Mother Aisha reminds us of this warning: "The Messenger of Allah forbade wisaal out of mercy to Muslims . . ."[66]

### b. Fasting for life

Islam is an easy religion, the rituals of which can be undertaken by anybody. There are no decrees in Islam that people cannot follow. Moderation is always highly valued and excess is prohibited in Islam. Fasting every day throughout one's life may bring about some negative consequences. It can weaken the body of the faster and this may impede everyday activities of their personal and social life. On the other hand, the body of the person who fasts in this way may become accustomed to continuous fasting and therefore he may not be able to enjoy the full benefits of fasting. These are some reasons why the

[66] al-Bukhari, Sawm, 20; Muslim, Siyam, 60; Abu Dawud, Sawm, 24; at-Tirmidhi, Sawm, 62.

Prophet forbade believers to fast every day and said this kind of fasting will not be accepted.[67]

### c. Fasting on the Doubtful Day

The Doubtful Day (Yawm al-Shakk) corresponds to the day right before Ramadan. The Noble Prophet forbade believers to fast on this day. The wisdom behind this may be the fact that the Prophet wanted believers to prepare for the fast of Ramadan or that he wanted them to investigate when the exact beginning and end of the acts of worship were so as to prevent any possible change. If it were customary to fast on the Doubtful Day, then the first day of Ramadan would change. What follows are two of the reports concerning this issue. Reported by Ammar ibn Yasir, the Prophet said, "Whoever fasts on the Doubtful Day, they have disobeyed Abu'l-Qasim (the Messenger of Allah)."[68] In another tradition the Prophet said, "None of you should fast a day or two before the month of Ramadan unless they are continuing their voluntary fasting."[69] So, this second tradition verifies that a person

---

67 al-Bukhari, Sawm, 57; Muslim, Siyam, 186; an-Nasai, Siyam, 71; Ibn Maja, Siyam 28.

68 al-Bukhari, Sawm, 11; at-Tirmidhi, Sawm,3; an-Nasai, Siyam, 37

69 al-Bukhari, Sawm, 14; Muslim, Siyam, 21; at-Tirmidhi, Sawm, 2; an-Nasai, Siyam, 31

can fast on the Doubtful Day if they have already begun a voluntary fast before that time.

## d. Fasting on the Eids and the Days of Tashriq

It is forbidden to fast on the first day of Eid al-Fitr—the fast-breaking feast, and the Eid al-Adha, the Feast of Sacrifice. It is also forbidden to fast on the Days of Tashriq, which are the three days following the first day of Eid al-Adha. On these four Days of Tashriq, the pilgrims in Mecca sacrifice their animals and Muslims all over the world commemorate festivities with their families and friends. These are the days of feast and happiness. Muslims should not fast on these days as this would mean that they would not be able to attend the festivities and share their happiness with other Muslims. Therefore, our beloved Prophet forbade Muslims to fast on these days, saying that these days are banquet tables prepared for people by Allah the Almighty. Uqba ibn Amir relates that the Prophet said, "The Day of Arafat, the Eid al-Adha and the Days of Tashriq are our festivals. These are the days of eating, drinking and remembering Allah."[70] Abu Sa'id reported: "The Messenger of Allah forbade fasting on these two days: Eid al-Fitr and Eid al-Adha."[71]

---

70 al-Bukhari, Eidain, 25; Abu Dawud, Sawm, 49; at-Tirmidhi, Sawm, 58

71 al-Bukhari, Adaahi, 16; Muslim, Siyam, 141; Abu Dawud, Sawm, 48; Ibn Maja, Siyam, 36.

## e. Fasting exclusively on Fridays

Friday is the day of festivity for Muslims. It is forbidden by Allah's Messenger to single out this day for fasting. He says, "Do not single out the night before Friday among the nights for worship and do not single out Friday among days for fasting except for anyone among you who is observing a fast that is customary to them."[72]

## f. Fasting at the time of menstruation and during postnatal bleeding

Women who are menstruating or experiencing postnatal bleeding are exempt from the responsibility of fasting in Ramadan. They do not fast and they do not perform their Daily Prayers. But, they must make up for the days of fasting they missed in Ramadan. Mu'adh ibn Jabal reports a tradition concerning this issue: "I asked mother Aisha why a woman with menstruation redeems the days of Ramadan fast she missed, but not the Daily Prayers. She answered: 'When we were with Allah's Messenger, he told us to redeem the fasts we missed during menstruation. He gave no orders concerning the Daily Prayers."[73]

---

[72] Muslim, Siyam, 148; Abu Dawud, Sawm, 50; at-Tirmidhi, Sawm, 41.

[73] Abu Dawud, Tahara, 104; an-Nasai, Hayd, 17; Ibn Hanbal, Musnad, 6/32.

# What is the significance of the pre-dawn meal (*sahur*)?

## a. Can one fast without having a pre-dawn meal?

Sahur is the meal that those who are fasting eat between midnight and the beginning of the dawn. Allah's Messenger recommended believers to partake of the pre-dawn meal even if it was just a morsel of food, saying that there is blessing in it and angels would pray to Allah on behalf of them. As reported by Abu Sa'id al-Khudri, Allah's Messenger said, "The pre-dawn meal is a blessed meal, do not neglect it, even if it is a mouthful of drink, for Allah and the angels bless those who observe it."[74]

Sahur means waking up at night or being awake before dawn. The time of sahur is the most blessed and fruitful time of the day. Indeed, it is blessed and fruitful in many ways: The person who partakes of the pre-dawn meal observes the tradition of the Prophet while also attaining enough energy and strength for the fast and other forms of worship throughout the day ahead. The person who will fast prays and remembers Allah, psychologically preparing themselves for the fast. Sahur is the best time to supplicate, to perform Prayers, to glorify Allah and to recite the Qur'an, because good deeds observed at that hour of the night have been reported to be more welcome than the rest of the day.

[74] Ibn Hanbal, Musnad, 3/12, 32, 44, 99.

### b. Delaying the pre-dawn meal

One of the important points about the pre-dawn meal is that it is recommended to delay it until shortly before the time of the Morning Prayer. This shows the mercy and compassion that the Prophet had for his community. Some people may suffer much from hunger and may not be able to bear fasting over an extended time. So, delaying the pre-dawn meal is a mercy for them, as it shortens the time of fasting. On the other hand, getting up for the pre-dawn meal earlier in the night may cause the believer to miss Morning Prayers. It is easier to partake of this meal shortly before dawn and then to perform the Morning Prayer after the adhan (the call for Daily Prayers) or when the time is due. Thus, it is not possible to miss the Prayer time. Concerning this issue, Allah's Messenger said, "My community will always remain in a good state so far as they hurry in the breaking of the fast and delay in the pre-dawn meal."[75]

## What are the teachings of the Prophet while breaking the fast?

### a. Breaking the fast right away

It is the tradition of the Noble Prophet to hasten to break the fast as soon as the call for the Evening Prayer (Maghrib) begins. Even though there is a short time to perform the

75 Abu Dawud, Sawm, 21; Ibn Hanbal, Musnad, 2/450.

Evening Prayers between the adhan of the Evening Prayer and the adhan for the Night-time Prayer ('Isha), Allah's Messenger used to break his fast first and then perform the Evening Prayers. This is a sign of his mercy and compassion toward people. The deep sense of compassion found in Islam would never allow people who have remained hungry the whole day to be forced to wait longer than necessary when it is time to break the fast. Therefore, our beloved Prophet urged his community to hasten in breaking the fast and thus gave the iftar meal a priority over Prayers. He said: "People are in a good state as long as they continue to hurry in breaking the fast."[76]

## b. Breaking the fast with water or dates

Breaking the fast with a sip of water or by eating a date is also the Sunnah, or Practice, of the Prophet. He used to break his fast with dates if there were any and with water if there were no dates. Then, he would perform the Evening Prayer. Anas ibn Malik reported: "Allah's Messenger used to break the fast with a few fresh dates before performing the Evening Prayer. If there weren't any fresh dates, he would break his fast with dried dates. If there weren't any dried dates, then he would drink a few sips of

[76] al-Bukhari, Sawm, 45; Muslim, Siyam 48; at-Tirmidhi, Sawm, 13; Ibn Maja, Siyam, 24; ad-Darimi, Sawm, 11.

water."[77] Sulayman ibn Amir reports that Allah's Messenger said: "When one of you is fasting, they should break their fast with dates; but if they cannot get any, then they should break their fast with water, for water is purifying."[78]

### c. Making a supplication at the time of breaking the fast

The supplications of some people are accepted and they are not turned away. Those who open their hands and supplicate to Allah at the time of breaking the fast are among those whose supplications are accepted, for Allah's Messenger said, "There are three categories of people whose supplications will not be rejected: the person who observes the fast until it is time to break it, a righteous ruler, and the person who has been wronged."[79] Allah's Messenger used to supplicate at the time of breaking the fast mostly as follows: "O Allah, I have fasted for Your sake, I have broken my fast with Your provisions. The thirst is gone and the veins are wet again. God willing, the reward is established, too."[80]

---

77 Abu Dawud, Sawm, 21; at-Tirmidhi, Sawm, 10; Ibn Hanbal, Musnad, 3/164.

78 Abu Dawud, Sawm, 21; at-Tirmidhi, Sawm, 10; Ibn Maja, Siyam, 25; ad-Darimi, Sawm, 12.

79 at-Tirmidhi, Daawat, 128, 130.

80 Abu Dawud, Sawm, 22.

## d. What is the significance of hosting *iftar* meals?

Hosting iftar meals during Ramadan is considered to be a good deed and a tradition that should not be neglected. Allah's Messenger says, "The person who hosts an iftar meal for another will earn a reward equivalent to the reward of the person who fasts without detracting from the reward of the latter."[81] Those who fast enjoy happiness and their hearts rejoice at the time of iftar (breaking the fast), but they will get the true reward when they reach Allah on the Day of Resurrection.[82] The Holy Prophet says: "There are two joys for the person fasting: One of them is when they break their fast, and the other is when they reach Allah."[83]

Allah will reward those who give even a date or an olive to a passerby who is fasting. Feeding a person who endures hunger and thirst for Allah is certainly a blessed action. It is reported that angels pray for the host while a guest stays at the dining table.

On the Doomsday Allah will say to some people "O children of Adam, I asked you for food and you fed Me not. They will say: 'O Lord! How can I feed You when

---

81 at-Tirmidhi, Sawm, 82; Ibn Maja, Siyam, 45.

82 al-Munziri, al-Targhib wal-Tarhib, 2/144.

83 al-Bukhari, Sawm, 2; Muslim, Siyam, 152; at-Tirmidhi, Sawm, 54; an-Nasai, Siyam, 41; Ibn Maja, Siyam, 1.

You are the Lord of the worlds?' Allah will say: 'Did you not know that My servant asked you for food and you fed him not? Did you not know that had you fed him you would surely have found (the reward for doing so) with Me?'"[84] There are splendid palaces in Paradise for those who talk sweetly, feed people, and perform the Prayers while everybody else is asleep.

There is more virtue in inviting friends and relatives to iftar than in giving alms. In order to emphasize the importance of feeding people, Ali ibn Abi Talib said, "One loaf of bread that I give to friends is more valuable than five that I give to the poor. A meal eaten with friends is better than paying for a slave to gain his freedom."

## Should one first perform the evening prayer or break the fast?

If the person fasting is sure that the time of Evening Prayer (Maghrib) has started, they should break their fast with something such as date or water first, and then perform the Prayer.

Eating the iftar meal quickly and then performing the Prayer is also possible. However, believers must be cautious not to delay the Prayer because of the delicious food on the dining table. Performing the Prayers in the earlier part of the prescribed duration of time is the most suit-

---

84 Muslim, Birr wa Sila, 43.

able way. Therefore, it is advisable to perform the Evening Prayer shortly after breaking the fast. On the other hand, some scholars are of the opinion that it is reprehensible (makruh) to perform Prayers first when the meal is ready. They argue that the mind of the person fasting may become occupied with food while performing the Prayers and hence the Prayer may not be performed appropriately. It is possible to have the meal first if this does not delay the Prayer. Yet, as mentioned above, performing the Prayer after breaking the fast with something light, so as not to cause any delay in the Prayer, is more in line with the recommendations of the Prophet. Thus, the person fasting will break their fast in time without having delayed the Evening Prayer, as recommended by the Messenger of Allah, peace and blessings be upon him.

## What are some prayers that can be said at the time of breaking the fast?

Saying prayers at the time of breaking the fast is one of the traditions of the Noble Prophet. Here are three well-known prayers for iftar:

ذَهَبَ الظَّمَأُ وَابْتَلَّتِ الْعُرُوقُ وَثَبَتَ الْأَجْرُ إِنْ شَاءَ اللهُ تَعَالَى

(The thirst is gone and the veins are wet again and the reward has been established, Allah willing). (Abu Dawud, Siyam 22)

اَللّٰهُمَّ إِنِّى لَكَ صُمْتُ وَبِكَ اٰمَنْتُ [وَعَلَيْكَ تَوَكَّلْتُ]
وَعَلَى رِزْقِكَ أَفْطَرْتُ

O Allah! I fasted for You and I believe in You [and I put my trust in You] and I break my fast with Your sustenance. (Abu Dawud, Siyam 22)

أَفْطَرَ عِنْدَكُمُ الصَّائِمُونَ وَأَكَلَ طَعَامَكُمُ الْأَبْرَارُ
وَصَلَّتْ عَلَيْكُمُ الْمَلَائِكَةُ

(May it please Allah that the fasting people may have iftar at your house and pious people may enjoy the hospitality of food provided by you. May the angels invoke blessings upon you with their prayers!) (Abu Dawud, At'ima 54)

## What about the *Tarawih* Prayer?

The word "tarawih" is the plural form of the Arabic word "tarwiha," which means to rest or relax. The name comes from tarwiha, or the rests, that are usually performed after every four cycles of this twenty-cycle Prayer performed after the Night Prayers ('Isha) in Ramadan. Tarawih is the plural form of tarwiha and was later used to mean the voluntary Prayer performed on the evenings of Ramadan.

Allah's Messenger encouraged his Companions to perform the Tarawih Prayer saying, "Whoever performs Tarawih Prayers at night the whole month of Ramadan out of sincere faith and hoping for a reward from Allah, then all their previous sins will be forgiven."[85]

The following incident provides clues about the conduct of the Prophet concerning the Tarawih Prayer: Allah's Messenger had a small hut near the Masjid an-Nabawi, which he used for i'tikaf (retreat). It is reported that on the last ten days of Ramadan he left this small hut for a few nights and led both the Night Prayer and the Tarawih Prayer in congregation. Seeing his Companions' enthusiasm he led the Night Prayer and retreated to his cell and did not come out to lead the Tarawih Prayer. Hoping that the Prophet would come out, people waited at the masjid and even began to cough so as to wake him up if he were asleep. The Prophet came out at the time of the Morning Prayer and addressed those waiting there: "I'm aware of your desire to perform Tarawih Prayer. There is nothing to hinder me from leading you in performing it. But because I was afraid that the Tarawih Prayer should be made compulsory for you and you might not be able to carry it out, I did not come out to lead you. Now, go home. The most virtuous Prayers except the obligatory (fard) ones are those performed at home."[86]

Tarawih was practiced by the Prophet as an example of an act of worship to be carried out by all believers.

[85] al-Bukhari, Salat al-Tarawih, 1; Muslim, Salat al-Musafirun, 174.

[86] al-Bukhari, Salat al-Tarawih, 2; Muslim, Salat al-Musafirun, 178.

The Tarawih Prayer consists of twenty cycles. It is performed after the Night Prayer ('Isha) and before Witr, the final Night Prayer. The Tarawih Prayer should be prayed in a congregation, and consists of ten salaams with the actual resting (tarwiha) being done five times. That is, after every two cycles there is a salaam and after every four cycles a rest. However, this Prayer can be performed by giving a salaam after every four cycles. Following the fifth rest, the Witr Prayer is then performed in congregation.

Allah's Messenger underscores the importance of performing the Tarawih Prayers and confirms that it is sunnah to perform it by saying, "Allah ordained fasting in the month of Ramadan and I encouraged you to perform Tarawih Prayers as my sunnah (tradition). Whoever fasts in the month of Ramadan and performs the Tarawih Prayer out of sincere faith and in hope for a reward from Allah, all their sins will be forgiven and they will be as purified as they were at birth."[87] Imam Nawawi, a prominent scholar of Islamic jurisprudence, has emphasized that the Tarawih Prayer is the tradition of the Prophet as concluded by the consensus of scholars (ijma).[88]

As was mentioned earlier, according to a hadith reported by mother Aisha, the Prophet led the Tarawih Prayers for a few nights in Ramadan and then gave it up lest it

---

87 an-Nasai, Siyam, 40; Ibn Maja, Iqama, 173; Ibn Hanbal, Musnad, 1/191.

88 an-Nawawi, Majmu, IV/37.

were to become obligatory. Nevertheless, it is clear that he encouraged his Companions to perform this Prayer.

Caliph Umar ibn al-Khattab, may Allah be pleased with him, ordered the believers to perform a twenty-cycle Tarawih Prayer in congregation in order to prevent disorder, for previously some Companions used to perform it individually and still others in congregation at the masjid. Umar ibn al-Khattab had Ubayy ibn Ka'b[89] lead the congregation in a twenty-cycle Tarawih Prayer and none of the Companions opposed this. Following this agreement and the practice of Companions, it was performed as twenty cycles at the masjid during the caliphate periods of Uthman and Ali (may Allah be pleased with them both) and the practice of twenty cycles has continued up to the present.[90]

## Does fasting mean only abstaining from food and drink?

Those who fast are required not only to abstain from food and drink, but also to avoid all kinds of bad deeds along with the desires of the carnal soul in order to get the full benefits and rewards of fasting. Those who fast must cer-

89 Caliph Umar ibn al-Khattab had Ubay ibn Ka'b lead the congregation, for Ibn Ka'b had led the Tarawih Prayer at the time of the Prophet as well.

90 Ayni, al-Binaya, 2/660; al-Mawsuat al-Fiqhiyya, 27/141.

tainly refrain from every kind of evil and be aware of any action that may lead to sin. Therefore, observing the fast does not mean only staying hungry and thirsty. People, especially those who observe the fast, must protect all their limbs against sins and act very cautiously, as if they were walking in a minefield, in order to protect themselves during this month. In short, they need to armor their hands, feet, head, and ears against the arrows of Satan and try not to be influenced by these.

## What is the fast of the eyes?

The eyes are among the most important organs Allah has bestowed upon human beings. The eyes enable people to see and appreciate the outside world and to think about it. The eyes are channels of perception for both the brain and the heart. They are, so to speak, doors to the mind and the spirit. People should restrain their eyes, especially when fasting, from unlawful and forbidden looks, which are like poisonous arrows and which may lodge in the heart. The Prophet indicates the sins that may be committed by the eyes, saying, "Unlawful looks are one of the poisonous arrows of the cursed Satan. Whoever gives that up for fear of Allah, He will reward that servant of His with a faith, the sweetness of which they will feel in their heart."[91]

---

[91] Hakim, Mustadrak, 4/314.

## What is the fast of the tongue?

Those who fast must restrain their tongue from lies, backbiting, and slander. They must also refrain from obscene language, swearing, and quarrels. The tongue must be occupied with recitation of the Qur'an and other books that will make the believer think about the Hereafter and the glorification of Allah. People who are fasting should avoid fighting or bickering with others, and they should not abase themselves by rising to the bait that others may try to throw in their way. Those who are truly fasting should say that they are fasting and therefore they will not respond or retaliate. They should not forget what Allah's Messenger said: "Fasting is a shield for believers. On the day you fast, do not use obscenity, nor yell at others, nor act ignorantly toward them. However, if anyone abuses you verbally or attempts to draw you into a fight with them, say 'I am fasting.'"[92]

People that do not control their tongue and continue to cause problems, even when they are fasting, i.e., people who think that fasting is only hunger, will be deprived of the benefits of and the rewards for observing the fast. Their only benefit will be hunger and thirst. On one occasion, the Noble Prophet said: "Allah has no need for the person who does not stop from false talk or stop from acting upon false talk to abstain from food and

[92] al-Bukhari, Sawm, 2; Muslim, Siyam, 161; Abu Dawud, Sawm, 25; at-Tirmidhi, Sawm, 54.

drink."[93] Again, on another occasion, Allah's Messenger said: "Many an observer of fasting will not receive any reward from their fast but the pain of hunger, and many a night worshipper will not receive any reward from their prayer but the loss of sleep."[94]

## What is the fast of the ears?

The ears, which are gifts to humanity from Allah, should be prevented from hearing false talk, backbiting, slander, and obscene words. Believers should leave places where such things are to be heard, for if something is improper to utter, then it is also improper to listen to it. This sacred decree of the Qur'an verifies that listening to false talk is unbecoming:

سَمَّاعُونَ لِلْكَذِبِ أَكَّالُونَ لِلسُّحْتِ

(which means: "They are the listeners of lies, devourers of what is forbidden . . ." [al-Maedah 5:42].)

## Should you recite the Qur'an more while fasting?

The Qur'an, which shows the believers the right way, is a book that must be read and reflected on all the time. The need for the Qur'an is like the need for air, water and bread.

93 al-Bukhari, Sawm, 8; Abu Dawud, Sawm, 25; at-Tirmidhi, Sawm, 16; Ibn Maja, Siyam, 21.

94 Ibn Maja, Siyam 21.

The Noble Prophet dedicated his whole life to drawing the attention of people to the Qur'an. He often recited it and had his Companions recite it while he was listening. He used to pay extra care to reading it, especially when he was fasting. Believers should follow this example of the Noble Prophet and dedicate hours to the recitation of the Qur'an and study it during Ramadan in order to be illuminated by its glowing atmosphere. The importance of reciting the Qur'an during Ramadan has often been underscored. Allah's Messenger used to be occupied with the Qur'an in Ramadan more than at any other time. He used to read it and reflect upon it, for this was the month in which Allah had revealed it. Every night in Ramadan Allah's Messenger would recite the Qur'an with the Archangel Gabriel. During every Ramadan they would recite the Qur'an to one another, from beginning to the end. They recited the whole of the Qur'an twice shortly before the Prophet's death. Ibn Abbas relates this in the following tradition: "Allah's Messenger was the most benevolent among people. His benevolence increased markedly during the month of Ramadan when Archangel Gabriel met him every night in order to recite the Holy Qur'an with him. Allah's Messenger was more charitable than the fast moving winds that bring the blessing of torrential rain."[95]

---

[95] al-Bukhari, Bad al-Wahy, 5, 6; Sawm 7; Manaqib, 23; Muslim, Fadail, 48, 50.

# Chapter 4
# Some Principles and Fundamentals of Fasting

## For whom is the fast obligatory?

Fasting in the month of Ramadan is obligatory upon every Muslim, male or female, who fulfills the following qualifications:

Being a Muslim: Fasting is obligatory for those who have accepted Islam. Non-Muslims cannot be forced to observe the fast.

Being a sane individual who has reached puberty: Another requirement for fasting is that the believer must have reached puberty and must be sane. Minors under the age of puberty are not obligated to observe the fast. Minors and those who are insane are exempted from the obligation of the other acts of worship as well. Allah's Messenger points to this fact in a tradition: "The responsibility has been lifted from three people; the minor, until he reaches the age of puberty; the insane person, until he recovers; and the sleeping person, until he wakes up."[96]

Being physically fit and not traveling: Fasting is not obligatory for those who are ill or those who are on a journey. The infinite compassion and mercy of Allah has lifted the responsibility of observing the fast in the month of Ramadan from the unhealthy, the ill, and the traveler. However, if they observe the fast despite being exempted, it will be valid. If they do not observe the fast during Ramadan because of their exemption, then they will make it up later when the reason for their exemption no longer exists (i.e. they are once again healthy or not traveling any longer). In the Qur'an, Allah the Almighty says:

أَيَّامًا مَعْدُودَاتٍ فَمَنْ كَانَ مِنْكُمْ مَرِيضًا أَوْ عَلَى سَفَرٍ فَعِدَّةٌ مِنْ
أَيَّامٍ أُخَرَ وَعَلَى الَّذِينَ يُطِيقُونَهُ فِدْيَةٌ طَعَامُ مِسْكِينٍ فَمَنْ تَطَوَّعَ
خَيْرًا فَهُوَ خَيْرٌ لَهُ وَأَنْ تَصُومُوا خَيْرٌ لَكُمْ إِنْ كُنْتُمْ تَعْلَمُونَ

(which means: "The fast is for a fixed number of days. If any of you be so ill that he cannot fast or is on a journey, then he must fast the same number of days on other days. But for those who are no longer able to fast, there is redemption granted by feeding a person in destitution for each day missed or by giving him the same amount of money. Better yet is for he who volunteers greater good by either giving

[96] al-Bukhari, Hudud, 22; Abu Dawud, Hudud, 17; at-Tirmidhi, Hudud; Ibn Maja, Talaq, 15; Ibn Hanbal, Musnad, 6/100, 101, 144.

more or fasting in case of recovery, and that you should fast when you are able to, is better for you, if you but knew the worth of fasting" [al-Baqarah 2:184].)

## What are the situations in which fasting is not required?

As we saw above, the obligation of fasting is dependent on the fulfillment of some requirements. Thus, people who fall into one of the following categories are not responsible for fasting in Ramadan:

Being on a journey: Those who are on a journey are not obliged to observe the fast, as this may be beyond their capacity. Those who are on a journey will make up for the fast at a later time, one day for each day missed; however, if they observe the fast despite their exemption, then, their fast is valid.

Illness: People who are ill so that their health is likely to be affected by the observance of the fast may postpone the fast for the time that they are unwell, making it up at a later date, one day for a day.

The term illness needs to be further clarified. It can be defined as a state in which the physical organs of the body do not work and in which they are not able to respond to the stimulants of the environment. Therefore, both a serious health problem that is difficult to cure and a trivial ailment can be accepted as an illness. Therefore, a physician who understands the requirements of fasting should be consulted in order to decide whether an illness requires breaking the fast or not. If a person who is not seriously ill is to break the fast by saying that they are seriously ill, then they are responsible for that before the Almighty Allah.

Pregnantwomenormotherswhoarebreast-feeding:Pregnant women or mothers who are breast-feeding their children may postpone their fast if its observance is likely to endanger their own health or that of their infants. They must make up the fasts they miss at a later time, one day for a day. Furthermore, women who are menstruating must postpone the fast until they have finished the menstruation and then make up for it, one day for a day.

Old age: Believers who are too old and weak to undertake the obligation of the fast and to bear its hardships are exempted from fasting. However, they must feed an indigent person for each of the days missed or offer the value in money for an average full meal per person per day.

Excessive hunger and thirst: People whose physiological and psychological health will be impaired in the case of excessive hunger or thirst may postpone the fast to a later date and make up for it, one day for a day.

Compulsion (Ikrah): Ikrah means forcing someone to break the fast. If someone threatens a person fasting that they will kill that person or harm them in some way if they do not cease from fasting if it is possible for this to happen, then the person fasting is allowed to break the fast.

## When and how should the intention to fast be made?

Making the intention to fast is an important stipulation for fasting. Fasting without having made the intention beforehand is not acceptable. Therefore, it is important to know when and how to make the intention for fasting.

Fasts are divided into two categories considering the timing of the intention to fast:

1. Intention made from the evening until approximately three quarters after sunrise: These are the fast of Ramadan, the supererogatory fasts, and avowed fasts to be observed at pre-determined days.

The intention for these fasts can be made either the night before the fast begins or in the morning until approximately three quarters after sunrise. Nevertheless, it is more virtuous to make the intention at night following the pre-dawn meal.

The permission to make intention until approximately three quarters after sunrise is dependent upon the condition that the person fasting does not eat or drink anything nor do anything that invalidates fasting before this time, as the fast begins following the dawn. Making the intention to fast after doing something that invalidates the fast is not acceptable.

2. Intention made at night until the dawn before the fast begins: The fasts in this category are those that are to

make up Ramadan fasts that have been missed before (qada), all kinds of expiatory (kaffara) fasts, and fasts to make-up for the supererogatory fasts that were broken and those in fulfillment of vows. Because there is no predetermined time to observe these fasts, it is essential to make the intention for them before dawn.

As we saw above, it is possible to make the intention for the Ramadan fast from the evening until approximately three quarters after sunrise, while normally the intention is made after having the pre-dawn meal. However, if a person does not get up before dawn to have the pre-dawn meal, then they can make their intention until approximately three quarters after sunrise, on the condition that they do not act in a way that will invalidate the fast from dawn until they have made their intention to fast.

Those people who do not want to get up during the night to have the pre-dawn meal can make their intention to fast for the next day before going to bed. Rising in the night is not mandatory for making one's intention.

The person fasting is not required to make the intention to fast aloud. The intention is made in the heart. That is, if a person happens to think that they will fast the next day this is accepted as their having made an intention. Getting up for the pre-dawn meal is, therefore, accepted as intention for the fast of the next day. Yet, it is better to utter the intention aloud as well. Therefore, believers who are eligible for observing the fast should make the intention both in their heart and with their tongue, saying: "I intend to observe the Ramadan fast tomorrow." It is obligatory to make the intention for each day of the fast separately.

## Which actions do not invalidate the fast?

- If anyone, through forgetfulness, does something that would ordinarily invalidate the fast, the fast is not nullified provided that the person stops doing that action the moment that they realize what they are doing.
- If you see a weak or an elderly person forgetfully eat or drink something, it is better not to remind them of their fast for this is the sustenance offered by the All-Merciful Allah through their forgetfulness, because of their weakness. If the person is not weak or old, then it is better to warn them.
- Wet dreams do not invalidate the fast.
- Pecking or touching one's spouse does not nullify the fast provided that one has self-control and there is no ejaculation of semen. It is, however, reprehensible (makruh) to kiss or touch one's spouse if they are not sure that they can control themselves. One should also be careful to not swallow the saliva of the beloved person as this

requires both make-up day (qada) and expiation (kaffara).

- Ejaculation of semen as a result of looking at or thinking about someone without physical contact. However, even if one fulfills the minimum conditions of fasting by abstaining from food, drink, and sexual intercourse from dawn until sunset, a person who is fasting should aim to control their desires by occupying their heart with nothing else but Allah and protect all their limbs against every kind of evil through the training of their will power during the fast. In this way, they observe the fast in a perfect manner by refraining from lustful looking at or thinking about what is unlawful during the fast.
- Having the bath after dawn following wet dreams or marital relations at night.
- Things that are part of daily living, such as swallowing saliva and inhaling mucus.
- Water that leaks into the ears when swimming or bathing.
- Unintentional inhalation of cigarette smoke or the smoke other pleasure-giving substance.
- Swallowing or sniffing dust, dirt, flies, and so on. The inadvertent swallowing of a few tear drops or drops of perspiration from the face does not nullify the fast, provided that it is not too much

and the salt is not felt in every part of the mouth. Intentional swallowing of such perspiration invalidates the fast.

- The inadvertent swallowing of the tiny morsels of food left between the teeth. If the morsel is larger than a chickpea, it nullifies the fast.
- Chewing something like a sesame seed or wheat grain, without tasting it in the throat.
- Giving blood.
- Coloring the eyelids or using kohl.
- Things that are absorbed through skin pores. Creams that are applied to the skin and water that is used for cleaning and washing up do not nullify the fast, for these are absorbed through the pores, not the mouth or nose.
- A medicine applied to the outer body, provided that it does not enter the body.

## Do injections and vaccinations invalidate the fast?

There are two kinds of channels or ways for something to enter the body:

a. Primary channels, such as the mouth, nose, ears, anus and vagina. There is a consensus among scholars that anything that enters the body through these channels invalidates the fast. So, any fluid or medicine that passes through throat, nose or anus nullifies the fast.

However, things that do not reach inside the body in this way, such as performing ghusl, pouring water over oneself, or submerging oneself in water, are not nullifiers.

b. Secondary channels, such as a cut or a wound on the skin. Again, there is an agreement that anything entering the body through these channels will nullify the fast. However, there is no agreement among Islamic scholars whether or not the fast is nullified if it is not known or when it is not certain that something has entered the body. If the person fasting is doubtful whether the thing has entered the body through the cut or the wound, then according to Imam Abu Yusuf and Imam Abu Muhammad the fast is not nullified, but according to Imam Abu Hanifa it is.

Apparently, the dispute between Imam Abu Hanifa and his two disciples is not about the essence of the matter, but the circumstance. That is, if it is certain that something has entered inside the body they are all in agreement that it nullifies the fast.

Similarly, any injections—whether for feeding or for medicinal purposes—nullify the fast, requiring only a make-up day (qada). In this case, it does not matter if the injection was intravenous or underneath the skin, or whether what was injected reaches the stomach. Accordingly, if it is possible for the sick (who already made the intention to fast the day) to delay their injections till the iftar meal, this is of course better for them.

## What is the status of certain reprehensible (*makruh*) and other actions with regard to invalidating the fast?

- According to some scholars, the use of wet or dry miswak (a special stick or root, usually from the arak tree, whose tip is softened and used to cleanse the teeth) does not break the fast. However, according to Imam Abu Yusuf, using a wetted miswak is undesirable.
- According to Imam Shafii, it is undesirable to use miswak in the afternoon. It is better to be cautious and not to use it while fasting.
- It is undesirable to use and waste too much water while performing ablutions.
- It is undesirable for a person fasting to taste food with the tip of the tongue without any good reason. But a dish may be tasted to decide if the seasoning is correct; this is done only on condition that it is not swallowed and if the household is too fussy about the food.
- It is undesirable for a person fasting to taste any food one wants to buy in order to understand whether it is good or not. According to some Islamic scholars, however, this is permissible if there is a probability that the person may be cheated.

- It is undesirable to chew gum while fasting.
- Donating too much blood and thus becoming too weak to go on fasting is undesirable. It is better to do this after the iftar meal.
- According to Imam Abu Hanifa, it is undesirable to take water inside the mouth and spit it out or to have a shower with cold water in order to lessen the heat and cool oneself. Such an act shows that one is finding the act of worship observed difficult and strenuous. According to Imam Abu Yusuf, however, this is not undesirable as it will help ease the difficulties of worship, and thus is not reprehensible.
- It is undesirable for spouses to kiss and fondle each other if they are not sure that they can control themselves.
- Those who fast can begin and go on fasting the following day after having had sexual intercourse without having made complete ablution (ghusl) first. However, it is undesirable to neglect making ghusl at night, if possible.
- It is not undesirable to sniff odors such as that of roses and musk. Also, it is not undesirable to color the eyelids or use kohl. However, it is undesirable for one to color the eyelids or lubricate the mustache as a form of make-up.

## What is the status of certain recommended (*mustahabb*) actions with regard to the fast?

The following are recommended to anyone fasting:

- Getting up for the pre-dawn meal at night. In Sahih al-Bukhari and Sahih Muslim it is reported that the Noble Prophet said, "Have your pre-dawn meal, for in that is a blessing." In another tradition he said, "Get the strength for the fast of the day by having the pre-dawn meal and the strength for nightly Prayers (Tahajjud) by having a nap at noon." The pre-dawn meal gives energy and strength and thus fasting becomes easier to observe.
- Delaying the pre-dawn meal and having it shortly before dawn and having the fast breaking meal as soon as possible after sunset. The Messenger of Allah says: "People will always remain in a good state of mind and body so long as they hurry in the breaking of the fast and delay the pre-dawn meal." In a hadith qudsi it is said: "The most sympathetic of My servants is the one who hastens most to have the iftar meal." The Noble Prophet used to break his fast before performing Evening Prayers. He would eat one or two dates, or drink a few sips of water if there were not any dates and then perform the Prayers. After the Prayers he would have the fast breaking meal. As for the time

of the pre-dawn meal, the following tradition reported by Zayd ibn Thabit can be taken as a guideline: "We had the pre-dawn meal with Allah's Messenger. Then, we performed the Morning Prayer." Anas ibn Malik then asked, "What was the time period between the pre-dawn meal and the Prayer?" Zayd ibn Thabit answered, "The equivalent of the time to recite 50 verses of the Qur'an." This corresponds to approximately 15 or 20 minutes. Scholars give the 69th and 77th chapters of the Holy Qur'an (al-Haqqah and al-Mursalat, respectively) as examples. Surahs al-Haqqah has 52 verses and al-Mursalat has 50.

Because of this tradition, scholars have decided that the pre-dawn meal should finish 15 or 20 minutes before the first light of dawn (imsak).

- Recite this supplication at the time of breaking the fast: Allahumma laka sumtu wabika amantu wa 'alaika tawakkaltu, wa'ala rizquka aftartu. It means: "O Allah, I have fasted for Your sake. I believed in You, and relied on You and I break my fast on Your provisions."
- Breaking the fast by eating something sweet like dates or drinking some water.
- Another important recommended action of the fast is that the one fasting should force all the parts of the body to fast just as the stomach does.

They should restrain their limbs and faculties, such as the eyes, ears, heart, and intellect from transient things and sins and lead them to their own duties of worship and servitude to Allah the Almighty. For example, they should restrain their tongue from telling lies, backbiting, and obscene talk and engage the tongue with recitation of the Qur'an, remembrance, and glorification of Allah (dhikr), peace and blessings for the Prophet, and asking for forgiveness (tawba and istighfar).

- It is possible to observe the fast in a perfect manner if one refrains from looking at what is unlawful and listening to falsehood and obscenity, and by engaging the eyes with the observation of the wonders created by the Almighty Allah and dedicating the ears to hearing the divine truth and the Qur'an. Immaculate virtues can be attained through this perfect fast. In a tradition Allah's Messenger says, "Whoever does not abandon falsehood in speech and action, Allah has no need of him abandoning his food and drink." In another tradition he says, "Five things invalidate the fast (that is, lessen the rewards and virtues it brings about): Telling lies, backbiting, slandering, false swearing, and lustful looks at what is unlawful." In order for the fast to be acceptable and valid, the believer should lower their gaze, safeguard their tongue, and abstain from listening to falsehood and obscenity, as well as controlling the rest of the body parts. Ibn Hajar says, "The complete and perfect fast means abstaining from all sins and everything that Allah has forbidden."

- Manners of fasting also include not eating too much at iftar or sahur; one of the wisdoms behind the fast is giving the body the ability to rest and relax for a while, as well as giving it an opportunity for annual renewal and rejuvenation. What is intended by the fast will be neglected if one rushes ardently to the dining table and fills the stomach to the limit after a day of being hungry and thirsty. Such an action is also harmful to the body, for the digestive system may not be able to respond to such a sudden attack. This excessiveness in eating will breed drowsiness and lethargy, and thus the believer will not make good use of themselves for the remainder of the night. Therefore, after fasting, one should not eat feverishly at the iftar and sahur table. Eating to satisfy the hunger is more relevant to the wisdom and purpose of fasting.
- All believers should worship more, be thankful to Allah the Almighty for the infinite bounties

He bestowed, and be more eager to do good deeds and help other people during the holy month of Ramadan. Reciting and listening to the recitation of the Qur'an is highly rewarded during this month. Therefore, those who can recite the Qur'an should recite it often and read it all the way through at least one time during this month. Those who cannot read it should go to mosques to listen to the recitation of the holy verses of the Qur'an by those who can recite the Qur'an by heart. Thus, holy Ramadan can be observed with the veneration and diligence it deserves.

## What do make-up days (*qada*) and expiation (*kaffara*) mean?

Make-up day (qada) consists of making up for each of the missed days of the obligatory fasts or the fasts that are invalidated unintentionally.

Expiation (kaffara) means fasting for two lunar months or sixty consequent days to make up a fast of Ramadan that is invalidated voluntarily or intentionally.

Considering the evidence for the necessity of expiation based on an event that took place at the Prophet's time, all Islamic scholars agree on the necessity of the expiatory fast for reckless and deliberate break of a fasting day in Ramadan.

It is a major sin to break the fast of Ramadan without any acceptable reason. Therefore, those who break the fast voluntarily are given a penance to fast sixty days, which is called expiation (kaffara) for violating the esteem and reverence of this holy month.

The expiation is required if one has marital relations, eats, or drinks intentionally during the fast of Ramadan. The sequence of the expiation reported in the tradition consists of freeing a slave, or if not possible, then fasting the days of two successive months. If this is not possible, then the expiation is to feed sixty needy people.

There are different opinions as to whether the same sequence should be followed or whether one should be allowed to choose from the types of expiation mentioned in the tradition of the Noble Prophet. According to the Hanafi School of Thought it is not a matter of choice but rather the sequence reported in the tradition should be followed. That is, the person who breaks the fast must fast for two consecutive months, as there are no slaves today. If this person is not able to fast two consecutive months, then they must feed sixty poor people for one day or feed a poor person for sixty days.

Feeding the poor as expiation for breaking the obligatory fast presents an important opportunity for helping the poor and thus securing social justice in a community. Expiation in this way serves as a penance for those who break the fast voluntarily and as a means of procuring brotherhood and solidarity in the community.

## What things invalidate the fast?

Like any other act of worship, fasting, which is obligatory during the month of Ramadan, has certain rules. Those things that nullify the fast, which form an important part of these rules, can be divided into two categories: Those that entail a make-up day and those that entail both a make-up day (qada) and expiation (kaffara).

## Which things necessitate a make-up day (*qada*)?

- Eating or drinking things that are not normally eaten by or that do not appeal to human beings, such as stones, soil, uncooked rice, dough, flour, and so on. Breaking the fast with one of these or something like these entails that the fast be made up, but not expiated.
- Eating unripe walnuts or swallowing almonds, hazelnuts or peanuts with the shell.
- Inserting suppositories or medicine into anus.
- Sniffing medicine.
- Dripping oil into the ear.
- Pouring something into the throat through a funnel.

- The absorption of something that is applied to a cut or wound on the head or belly.
- Swallowing rainwater, snow or hail unintentionally.
- The unintentional swallowing of water when taking ablution.
- Intentional inhaling of smoke. If the smoke inhaled intentionally is a pleasure-giving substance such as cigarette or amber smoke, then it requires expiation (kaffara) together with a make-up day (qada).
- The person fasting who is forced to have sexual relations must make up for the fast but does not need to expiate it. Forcing, here, means severe physical torture. After sexual intercourse as a result of intimidation, however, if one makes the intention to fast and then breaks the fast, this requires both a make-up day and expiation.
- If someone pours water into the throat of the person fasting while they are sleeping, the fast is invalidated and the person fasting needs to make up for it.
- Continuing to eat or drink something thinking that the fast has been invalidated after eating or drinking by mistake forgetfully. The fast is valid if the believer eats or drinks forgetting that they are observing the fast and stops abruptly when they remember they are fasting.

- Eating a morsel of food that has remained between the teeth and that is as large or larger than a chickpea.
- Voluntary vomiting, even if it is less than a mouthful.
- Involuntary vomiting, greater than a mouthful that goes back from the mouth to the stomach.
- Having sahur meal after its due time thinking that its time has not yet passed.
- Having iftar meal before sunset thinking that it is time to break the fast.
- Intentional or unintentional breaking of a supererogatory fast.
- Orgasm of man or woman as a result of kissing, hugging, or embracing.
- Eating or drinking during the daytime in Ramadan without having made the intention to fast entails a make-up day but not expiation, for expiation is not a penance for not observing the fast, but rather for breaking a worship that has begun. But negligence of fasting during the month of Ramadan is a major sin and it requires repentance.
- Swallowing somebody's saliva or a morsel of food that has been chewed by someone else or a morsel of food that one has chewed and removed from the mouth for a certain amount of time entails a make-up day and not expiation, as such

an act is not appealing to human beings. However, swallowing the saliva of a beloved person requires expiation, for it gives pleasure.

- Putting something wet inside one's private parts. Therefore, people who are fasting should be careful when washing after relieving themselves so as not to spread moisture to the inner parts of the private parts.
- Masturbation.
- Swallowing blood in the mouth. If the amount of blood is less than the saliva, this does not nullify the fast.

## Which things necessitate both make-up day and expiation?

Doing one of the following things voluntarily or without forgetting the fast requires both a make-up day and an expiation:

- Sexual intercourse.
- Eating or drinking something or taking medicine.
- Voluntarily swallowing rainwater, snow, or hail that has entered the mouth accidentally.
- Intentional smoking or snuffing tobacco or inhaling the smoke of any other pleasure-giving herb.
- Eating hard animal fat, dried meat, or uncooked meat.

- Swallowing something smaller than a sesame or wheat kernel that has remained between the teeth does not invalidate the fast. On the other hand, putting such a thing into the mouth and swallowing it nullifies the fast and entails expiation. However, chewing or grinding it with teeth without swallowing does not harm the fast even if this is undesirable. This invalidates the fast if its taste reaches the throat.
- Taking a morsel of food smaller than a chickpea out of the mouth and then returning it back to the mouth and eating it breaks the fast but does not necessitate expiation, for such an action is not normal or appealing.
- Swallowing saliva or spittle of one's spouse or beloved. This invalidates the fast and requires expiation, for it gives pleasure.

## What about the expiatory (*kaffara*) fast?

- The believer that has to expiate must observe the fast for two consecutive months. Therefore, they should be careful to choose a period of two months in which the expiatory fast will not be interrupted by an obligatory fast, such as that of Ramadan or days on which it is forbidden to fast. Otherwise, the expiator must start afresh and fast for sixty consecutive days.

- Although there is permission for travelers not to observe the fast in Ramadan, which is obligatory, the expiator has to go on fasting even if they are on a journey.
- Menstruation or post childbirth bleeding does not harm the consecutiveness of the expiatory fasts. Women will break the expiatory fast when menstruation or post childbirth bleeding begins and go on completing the rest of the expiatory fasting days afterwards.
- As mentioned before, expiation is not a penance for not observing an obligatory fast but for breaking a worship that has begun. Therefore, negligence of the fast of Ramadan without having made the intention to fast entails a make-up day but not expiation. However, negligence of the obligatory fasting days of Ramadan is a major sin and it requires repentance.

## Which situations obviate the need to perform expiation?

If a new situation such as menstruation or post childbirth bleeding, which entails make-up day but not expiation happens on the same day after the intentional breaking of the fast, which entails expiation, then the obligation of expiation is nullified. The same rule can be applied to situations such as the occurrence of illness during the day, as well.

Setting out on a journey, no matter whether it is necessary or not, and causing oneself to become ill voluntarily after intentionally breaking the obligatory fast does not obviate the obligation of expiating the fast.

## What does expiatory payment (*fidya*) mean?

People who are not able to fast because of constant illness or old age feed an indigent person for each of the fasting days they have missed. In Islamic terminology this is called fidya (expiatory payment). Just as in the case of expiation by feeding the poor, by paying fidya to the poor, too, the responsibility to fast in Ramadan is lifted from the physically disable, the poor are fed and thus social justice is restored. In the Holy Qur'an Allah says:

أَيَّامًا مَعْدُودَاتٍ فَمَنْ كَانَ مِنْكُمْ مَرِيضًا أَوْ عَلَى سَفَرٍ فَعِدَّةٌ مِنْ أَيَّامٍ أُخَرَ وَعَلَى الَّذِينَ يُطِيقُونَهُ فِدْيَةٌ طَعَامُ مِسْكِينٍ فَمَنْ تَطَوَّعَ خَيْرًا فَهُوَ خَيْرٌ لَهُ وَأَنْ تَصُومُوا خَيْرٌ لَكُمْ إِنْ كُنْتُمْ تَعْلَمُونَ

(which means: "The fast is for a fixed number of days. If any of you be so ill that he cannot fast or is on a journey, then he must fast the same number of days on other days. But for those who are no longer able to fast, there is redemption granted by feeding a person in destitution for each day missed or by giving him the same amount of money. Better yet is for he who volunteers greater good by either giving more or fasting in case of recovery, and that you should fast when you are able to, is better for you, if you but knew the worth of fasting" [al-Baqarah 2:184].)

## What is *i'tikaf* (retreat) and how should it be performed?

I'tikaf means to retreat to a mosque or any other place of worship in order to engage in worship and remembrance of Allah (dhikr) during the last ten days of Ramadan.

The Holy Qur'an indicates this religious act in the following verse:

وَلاَ تُبَاشِرُوهُنَّ وَأَنْتُمْ عَاكِفُونَ فِي الْمَسَاجِدِ

(which means: "…do not associate with your wives while you are in retreat in the mosques." [al-Baqarah 2:187].)

It is apparent in the sources of traditions that after the emigration to Madina Allah's Messenger used to retreat to the mosque for the last ten days of Ramadan and that he recommended the same to his wives. One of these traditions is as follows: "On the last ten days of Ramadan, Allah's Messenger used to spend the night worshipping. He used to wake up his family so that they could worship, as well. He would strive to worship more than he did at other times."[97]

In the proceedings of every-day life human beings forget the real cause for their being sent to this world. Actually, every believer needs to reflect on the meaning and the purpose of life. Observing i'tikaf for the last ten days of Ramadan, which is the month of mercy and forgiveness, provides the believer with an opportunity for reflection. Moreover, the fact that the Laylat al-Qadr (Night of Power), which is better than a thousand months, is concealed in the last ten days of Ramadan makes i'tikaf more important for believers. Although this useful tradition has been forgotten in recent years, it was a prevalent practice among believers in the past. In each town at least a few people would retreat to the mosques to continue this practice of the Prophet, peace and blessings be upon him.

Ataa ibn Abu Rabah, a prominent scholar of Islam, described the person who performs i'tikaf saying: "The man that retreats looks like a person who sits at the door of an exalted individual and says 'I will not leave or go.' He takes refuge in Allah's house of worship saying 'I will not leave from here unless He forgives me.'"

There are some rules and principles for retreat: It should be observed during the last ten days of Ramadan

---

[97] al-Bukhari, I'tikaf, 1, 6; Muslim, I'tikaf, 2, 7; at-Tirmidhi, Sawm, 71.

and in the most virtuous mosques. During the retreat nothing other than what is good should be spoken. There is no harm in talking about the things that do not lead to offense or transgression. Staying mute, thinking that this is worship, is reprehensible and undesirable. However, restraining the tongue from what is bad and indecent is accepted as a great worship. The person who does i'tikaf should go on reading and teaching the Holy Qur'an, the traditions of the Prophet, the noble life stories of Prophets, and texts of religious matters. They should wear clean clothes and use pleasant odors. They can also apply lubricants to their hair. A person that wants to make the retreat incumbent upon their soul should not only intend this with their heart, but also repeat the intention to do so audibly.

The numbered days of life gradually decrease and diminish. Therefore, passing some of the days of this transient world in worship and supplication to the Ever-Living and Eternal Creator of the universe with a pure heart and decent tongue is surely a blessing.

The person that performs retreat is accepted as having dedicated the whole of the time they spend in the mosque to worship and Prayers, for even when they are not performing Prayers they are ready and prepared for Prayers inside the mosque. Being in this state of readiness is like being in a state of performing worship.

Human beings can gain spiritual ascendancy through retreat. Their heart becomes enlightened and signs of worship and servitude gleam on their face.

## What should one do during the last ten days of Ramadan in search of the night of power?

Prophet Muhammad, peace and blessings be upon him, would spend most of the time in the mosque, devoting himself to worshipping the Almighty Allah and seeking the Laylat al-Qadr (Night of Power) in Ramadan. He would exert himself in the last ten days of Ramadan in a way that he did not exert himself on any other day and pray much. Allah the Almighty, the Most Merciful, has kept the precise day and time of the Night of Power hidden from the believers and encouraged them to take advantage of this fact, striving in their worship during the last ten days of Ramadan, while seeking the Night of Power.

The Night of Power is the most blessed night. It was on this night that the single most important event in history unfolded as Archangel Gabriel descended with the blessed book to reveal it to the Messenger of Allah. Emphasizing its importance, Allah the Almighty says:

وَمَا أَدْرَاكَ مَا لَيْلَةُ الْقَدْرِ

(which means: "and how would you know the value of the Night of Power?" [al-Qadr 97:2].) So valuable is this blessed night that the Qur'an devotes one chapter to it, saying:

لَيْلَةُ الْقَدْرِ خَيْرٌ مِنْ أَلْفِ شَهْرٍ

(which means: "The Night of Power is better than a thousand months" [al-Qadr 97:3].)

It possesses much good and blessing due to its merit and the great reward that awaits the sincere believer who does good deeds on this night. Angels descend from the Heavens during this night due to its countless blessings:

تَنَزَّلُ الْمَلَائِكَةُ وَالرُّوحُ فِيهَا بِإِذْنِ رَبِّهِمْ مِنْ كُلِّ أَمْرٍ

(which means: "Therein descend the angels and the Spirit by their Lord's permission with all decrees" [al-Qadr 97:4].)

Allah the Almighty describes this night as being imbued with. . . peace until the rise of the morn (al-Qadr 97:5). In various sayings, the Prophet described this night as serene, tranquil, and peaceful.

Muslims must be conscious of this bounty and acknowledge its magnitude. Sincere believers should stay up in prayer and remembrance of Allah during the ten nights on which the Night of Power could fall and hope to seek rewards from their Lord so that they shall be forgiven for their past sins.

# Chapter 5
# Charity in the Month of Ramadan

## What is the charity of fast breaking (*sadaqa al-fitr*)?

Fitr means "breaking the fast; the original constitution; or the nature of humans as created by Allah." Sadaqa al-fitr, the charity given by Muslims before the Eid Prayer (the Prayer marking the end of Ramadan), is called fitra. This small charity is imposed on every responsible Muslim who has the means for themselves and their dependents. Giving the charity of fast breaking is an act of worship that is related to property and is obligatory on every Muslim that possesses more than the prescribed amount of provisions after giving the charity. It is paid once yearly at the end of Ramadan before the Eid Prayer.

The charity of fast breaking is accepted as a provision for Ramadan Festival and considered as a fee for reaching this festival without any misfortune or trouble. In many blessed traditions Allah's Messenger commanded the believers to give the charity of fast breaking. Abdullah ibn Umar reported a tradition that "Allah's Messenger has commanded every slave, freeman, every man and woman, young and old to give the charity of fast breaking, one sa'a, (a unit of measurement that weighs about three kilos and 350 grams) of dates before the Eid Prayer."[98]

In another tradition, Abu Sa'id al-Khudri says, "We used to give during the time of the Messenger one sa'a of food, and our food was barley, raisins, dry milk, and dates."[99] In another tradition Allah's Messenger said, "Give the charity of fast breaking on behalf of those under your guardianship."[100]

Believers give the charity of fast breaking as a thanksgiving for life and existence, which are blessings bestowed upon human beings by Allah the Almighty. Therefore, the obligation of giving the charity of fast breaking does not depend on the condition of having observed the fast of Ramadan. That is, believers that do not observe the fast of Ramadan are also responsible for giving the charity of fast breaking. It is obligatory for every believer. How-

98 al-Bukhari, Zakat, 76; Muslim, Zakat, 12.

99 al-Bukhari, Zakat, 74.

100 al-Bayhaqi, Sunan Kubra, 4/161.

ever, although the non-faster gives the charity of fast breaking as a thanksgiving for having been given life and existence by Allah, the person fasting observes it as a thanksgiving for both the favor of life and existence and for having been able to observe the fast of Ramadan, which is itself a blessing.

As is related in a tradition the charity of fast breaking erases the flaws that are caused by unbecoming behavior during Ramadan and it perfects the fast. Also, it enables the poor to take part in the joys and delights of the festival.[101] Moreover, the charity of fast breaking is believed to be a means for the acceptance of the fast by Allah, as well as salvation and deliverance from the torment of death and the grave.

More people are obliged to give the charity of fast breaking than those who have to give zakat (the prescribed purifying alms), which is one of the five pillars of Islam. Thus, everybody who has the means gets a chance to enjoy the pleasure of giving something for the sake of Allah and to help provide better living conditions for the poor and needy in the community. Moreover, the poor are given a hand without having to beg for help and thus abase themselves. Hence, a new bridge of solidarity and friendship is constructed and made functional.

---

[101] Abu Dawud, Zakat, 17; Ibn Hanbal, Musnad, 2/277.

## Who is liable for the charity of fast breaking?

In order to be eligible for giving the charity of fast breaking a person should have the following characteristics:

Being a Muslim: Only Muslims are liable for giving the charity of fast breaking. According to Imam Shafii, however, a non-Muslim guardian of a Muslim must give the charity of fast breaking on their behalf.

Possessing more than the Prescribed Amount of Provisions (Nisab): Believers who will possess more than the prescribed amount of provisions after giving the charity of fast breaking are obliged to observe this act of worship. That is, they are eligible for giving the charity of fast breaking provided that they have a property worth of 85 grams of gold or 595 grams of silver. Unlike zakat (the prescribed purifying alms), the condition that the property should be of the kind that increases or gains value and that it should be possessed for a year is not applicable to the charity of fast breaking. According to the Shafii, Maliki and Hanbali schools of Islamic jurisprudence, it is not necessary to have the prescribed amount of provisions in order to be eligible for giving the charity of fast breaking. Those who possess enough food for the day and the night of the Eid as well as their basic needs are obliged to give the charity of fast breaking. If a believer loses his property or if the property decreases and becomes less than the prescribed amount, their obligation to give the charity of fast breaking is not nullified. However, if a believer that is eligible dies before giving it, their obligation is nullified. That is, the charity of fast breaking is not to be paid from their property. Nevertheless, it is better if the heirs pay it on behalf of the deceased.

Being sane and having reached the age of puberty are not prerequisites for giving the charity of fast breaking. According to Abu Hanifa and Abu Yusuf, the charity of fast breaking should also be given out of the property of the insane and the children under the age of puberty. The father gives the charity of fast breaking from the property of their wealthy children.

A believer must give the charity of fast breaking on behalf of children that are under their guardianship or for whom they are responsible. A Muslim that is eligible for giving the charity of fast breaking must also give the charity of fast breaking for those who are under their guardianship and who are not eligible to give the charity of fast breaking themselves. They must also give the charity of fast breaking on behalf of any children of their deceased son. Nevertheless, a person is not obliged to give the charity of fast breaking on behalf of those whom they take care of, including their parents, mature children, spouse, sisters or brothers or any other relatives. Although they take care of them, they are not under their custody. According to Imam Abu Hanifa, however, they can give the charity of fast breaking on behalf of these other people if they wish so.

Scholars of the other schools are of the opinion that a person that is eligible for giving the charity of fast breaking must also give it on behalf of any relatives for whom he is responsible, such as the parents or wife, if he has the means.

The charity of fast breaking (sadaqa al-fitr) becomes obligatory before the first day of the Eid al-Fitr—the festival celebrated at the end of the Ramadan fast, since it is attributed to the festivity. Therefore, the eligibility for the charity of fast breaking of those who die or become poor before the dawn of the festival is nullified. Anyone who is born or becomes a Muslim before the dawn of the first day of Eid is eligible for giving the charity of fast breaking.

## When is the charity of fast breaking to be paid?

The charity of fast breaking can be given beginning from the first day of Ramadan until the first day of the Eid. However, scholars have recommended that it be paid one or two days before the festival, as it is apparent in the traditions concerning this issue, that the main objective of this Islamic practice is to answer the needs of the poor before the festival. Delaying it to any time after the first day of the festival is undesirable. Nevertheless, the obligation is not nullified, even when it is postponed.

## How much should be paid for the charity of fast breaking?

As is mentioned before, traditions reveal that at the time of the Prophet the believers used to give one sa'a (3.350 kg) of the foodstuffs that were most consumed at that time, such as dates, barley, raisins, and so on. It is also reported that the Companions, including the Four Rightly-Guided Caliphs used to give ½ sa'a of wheat or one sa'a of dates, barley, or raisins as the charity of fast breaking. Taking the traditions and other reports into account, the scholars of canonical jurisprudence have agreed that the charity of fast breaking must be paid from the most commonly consumed foodstuff of the region. Also, the amount of the charity of fast breaking which was one sa'a at that time, must be enough to feed a poor person for one day.

It is to be noted that the kind of food that was prescribed was the main foodstuff of the time and that there was a ratio of value between each kind. Therefore, it can be concluded that the amount to be given should be determined in accordance with the living standards of the community and should be no less than enough to feed a poor person for one day. Obviously, it would neither be sufficient nor appropriate to give one sa'a of barley, wheat, raisins or dates as charity in our times.

Actually, it is better to take the amount of normal daily provision of a person as a base for giving the charity of fast breaking. However, the average living standards of the person who gives the charity of fast breaking and not that of the person who receives it should be taken into account. This is more relevant to the purpose of giving the charity of fast breaking. The following backs up such an approach. Concerning the expiatory payment for breaking an oath, Allah the Almighty says in the Holy Qur'an:

فَكَفَّارَتُهُ إِطْعَامُ عَشَرَةِ مَسَاكِينَ مِنْ أَوْسَطِ مَا تُطْعِمُونَ
أَهْلِيكُمْ أَوْ كِسْوَتُهُمْ أَوْ تَحْرِيرُ رَقَبَةٍ

(which means: "…for expiation, feed ten indigent persons,outoftheaveragefoodyoufeedyourfamilieswith" [al-Maedah 5:89].)

Moreover, the amounts prescribed in the traditions of the Prophet and the canonical resources are the minimum amounts. It is obvious that the main aim was to prevent the poor from asking for food and to help them so that they could enjoy the festivity. Therefore, a believer who is obliged to give the charity of fast breaking must give the amount of money they normally spend on food in a single day.

## How is the charity of fast breaking to be given?

Giving the charity of fast breaking is an act of worship and it is obligatory to make an intention before observing acts of worship. Therefore, the person who gives the charity of fast breaking must make the intention to do so first. The intention can be made when giving the charity of fast breaking or when setting it aside to be given later.

Making the intention means determining to give the charity of fast breaking for the sake of Allah in one's heart. Although making the intention in heart is valid, uttering the intention is also desirable. The person that gives the charity of fast breaking should present it as if they are giving a property to the poor, the needy, or students that have been left in their trust by the Almigthy. They do not need to say "This is the charity of fast breaking" when giving it.

It is better to give cash, because it may be difficult to figure out what the needs of the receivers of the charity are. If they receive cash, they can buy whatever they need for themselves. Yet, it can be given from the food-stuffs that are normally consumed by people of the region.

The charity of fast breaking must be given in person as a commodity into the hands of those who are eligible to receive it. That is, it cannot be the settlement of a past loan; this would be invalid.

## To whom is the charity of fast breaking given?

The charity of fast breaking can be given to those who are eligible to receive zakat (the prescribed purifying alms).

Therefore, people who are not eligible to receive zakat cannot receive the charity of fast breaking, either. A believer cannot give the charity of fast breaking to people who are understood to be wealthy, to their spouse, parents, grandparents, children, grandchildren or relatives for whom they are responsible for looking after.

When giving the charity of fast breaking, priority should be given to poor neighbors, relatives even if they live in a distant place, and students. The charity of fast breaking can be given to one person or to more than one person. However, it is better to give it to only one person so as to address the needs of this person. On the other hand, many people can give their charity to the same person if that person is eligible to receive the charity of fast breaking.

## How is the eid prayer to be performed?

The Eid Prayer is a two-rakat Prayer offered on the two annual religious festive days: the Eid al-Fitr (marking the end of Ramadan) and the Eid al-Adha (Festivity of Sacrifice). According to Hanafi school, conditions for the validity of the Eid Prayer are the same as those of the Friday Prayer except for the delivery of the sermon. That is, delivering sermon is obligatory for the Friday Payer to be valid, whereas it is sunna (a practice performed or advised by the Prophet but not obligatory) for the Eid Prayers.

Moreover, the sermon is delivered before the Friday Prayer, but after the Eid Prayer.

Eid Prayers are performed during the time immediately following the sunrise. There is no adhan unlike the Friday Prayer.

Another difference between the two Prayers is that, in each rakat of the Eid Prayer, the takbir (saying "Allahu Akbar"—Allah is the All-Great) is uttered for additional three times. These additional takbirs are obligatory for the Eid Prayers and they are uttered before reciting al-Fatihah, the opening chapter of the Qur'an, in the first rakat and after reciting al-Fatihah in the second rakat. When uttering takbir both arms are raised and then left down. In the first rakat, the hands are placed together and the Subhanaka prayer[102] is recited after the initial takbir. Then, additional takbirs are uttered together with the imam. The imam utters the takbirs out loud but the takbirs of the congregation are silent. With the utterance of the first "Allahu Akbar" the arms are raised and then left down. After a brief period (long enough to say "Subhana'llah" three times), the second takbir is uttered and the arms are raised and left down again and then this is repeated for the third time. Then, the congregation becomes silent

[102] Subhanaka'llahumma wa bi-hamdik. Wa tabaraka'smuk. Wa ta'ala jadduk. Wa la ilaha ghayruk. (Glory be to You, O Allah, and to You is the praise. Blessed is Your Name and most high is Your honor. There is no deity besides You).

and the imam begins to recite al-Fatihah aloud. After al-Fatihah he recites a portion from the Qur'an before bowing and prostration. After the second prostration, first the imam and then the congregation stand up for the second rakat. After reading al-Fatihah and an additional Qur'anic passage, the imam leads the congregation in extra four takbirs and they leave the arms down after the first three, and bow after the fourth one. Then they complete the Prayer.

After the Prayer the imam gives a sermon without sitting down. Unlike during Friday sermon, he utters tashrik takbirs saying "Allahu Akbar, Allahu Akbar, la ilaha illallahu wallahu Akbar. Allahu Akbar wa lillahilhamd," and the congregation repeat the words with him. He gives two sermons just as he does during the Friday sermon, sitting briefly between the two parts.

Takbirs are uttered on the way to the Prayer at the mosque. Takbirs are made silently at the Eid al-Fitr and loudly at the Eid al-Adha. In both Eids the takbirs are uttered out loud after reaching the mosque and before the Prayer.

# Chapter 6
# Fasting & Health

## Would Islam ordain a harmful practice; does fasting pose a medical risk?

Allah would not order human beings to do harmful things and certainly fasting is not harmful. Modern physicians keep asking themselves what is the secret of fasting that makes it so good as to deserve all this attention that has caused so many people to have fasted through the ages.

Fasting has been used in medicine for numerous medical reasons, including weight management, relief to the digestion system, and to lower lipid levels. Modern medicine states that the adrenalin and cortisone hormones in the body of a person who fasts are more easily able to mix with the blood. These hormones have positive effects upon cancer cells, as well. Thus, these hormones become a shield against cancer and hinder any increase in the number of cancer cells.

While observing the fast the body undergoes a period of maintenance. The layer of fat covering the interior organs is burned off, a new energy is generated, and the body gains a renewed power of resistance against ailments of the organs, such as the stomach, kidneys, heart, and liver. Fasting has positive effects on some kinds of diabetes, as well.

The liver, which has various tasks, also plays a role in digestion. During the fast it relaxes for 3-5 hours and stops storing nutrients. This enables it to produce globulins, which strengthen the defense system of the body. The muscles and secretion-producing cells in the stomach are able to rest for a few hours. Because the blood volume decreases during the fast the blood pressure is lessened and consequently the heart relaxes. Fasting is a useful treatment for those who have high blood pressure.

When the remnants of food are not fully consumed by the body, they pile up in the veins. The unconsumed food blocks the veins and causes hardening of the arteries, arteriosclerosis. When a person fasts, unconsumed food does not remain inside the body. That is, all the nutrients inside the body are consumed. Therefore, it is recommended that those who suffer from arteriosclerosis fast during other months, in addition to the fast during Ramadan.

While fasting, other organs of the body are able to rest, as well. Eating little and fasting are very important practices to ensure a healthy life. The payment of zakat (the prescribed purifying alms) is one way of purifying our worldly possessions. Similar to purifying the wealth through paying zakat, one purifies the body and the soul and protects them against disease through fasting. The Messenger pointed out to this fact saying "There is a zakat for everything and the zakat for the body is fasting."[103]

Most ailments are caused by over-eating. Over-eating and drinking are the main cause of poor health. People who overeat may fail to feel compassion for other beings. They become more aware of their ego and are thus more susceptible to being misled into doing wrong. All the ways and means that lead to sins must be obstructed beforehand. Hunger blocks the way of Satan. Satan flows inside the body like blood, and he can be stopped through fasting.

Fasting is also very beneficial for single adults who are inclined to the danger of sinning, as it impedes or lessens sexual desires.

## What are the medical benefits of fasting in Ramadan?

Muslims observe fasting in Ramadan not because it has medical benefits, but because it has been mandated by

---

[103] Tirmidhi, Daavat, 86; Ibn Maja, Siyam, 44.

Allah. Nevertheless, it is certain that it has many benefits, not only for the soul, but also for the body. Fasting has long been prescribed by physicians as a means of losing weight, relaxing the digestive system, and decreasing the amount of lipids in the blood. A complete diet, what is known as a "crash diet," has many negative influences upon the body. Fasting as is prescribed by Islam is different from this kind of diet. Fasting does not cause malnutrition and does not deprive the body of calories.

Calorie intake of people fasting during Ramadan is either in line with what is recommended or just below this. Fasting in Islam differs from diets and medicines that may be prescribed by a doctor in that it also involves the mind and the heart. Such a fast makes the believer think about the poor and provides them with an urge to help them immediately. This is something that is peculiar to the Islamic fasting.

Ramadan is a month of cross-examining oneself and of restraining the carnal desires; the continuation of such a state of mind at other times is something to be aimed. If this state of purity prevails even after Ramadan, the believer will be more able to lead a life full of happiness and good deeds.

Fasting in Islam is like a strict diet; the believer rises to have the sahur, which is an early breakfast, and do not eat or drink anything until sunset. They do not have lunch, or between-meal snacks. Thus, the body is able to rest.

Even after sunset it has been advised that the people who are fasting refrain from over-eating; in fact this is very hard to do, as the body has become accustomed to eating less, and therefore desires less.

The thirst experienced in Ramadan is not harmful to the body. It helps other fluids of the body become more concentrated. The dehydration caused by fasting is a system of conserving the other bodily liquids, which may lead the body to experience a healthier life, just as plants do.

Among the physiological benefits of fasting is the decrease in blood sugar, cholesterol and blood pressure. Actually, fasting is an ideal method for stabilizing diabetes which are not insulin dependent, obesity, and high blood pressure.

In 1994, fifty studies concerning the medical benefits of fasting were presented by both Muslim and non-Muslim scholars at the 1st International Congress on "Health and Ramadan" in Casablanca, Morocco.[104] None of these studies were able to come up with any findings concerning the negative effects of fasting upon body. As for those who suffer from rheumatoid arthritis and kidney stones, they are not obliged to fast.[105]

---

[104]The 1st International Congress on "Health and Ramadan," Casablanca, 1994.

[105]Toda M, Marimoto K.: Effects of Ramadan Fasting on the Health of Muslims. Nippon Eiselgaku Zasshi, 54 (4): 592-596.

Fasting has many psychological and moral benefits in addition to physiological benefits. People that fast during the month of Ramadan experience a state of peace and tranquility as a result of the pleasure they attain from the fast. They forget all kinds of resentments and ill feeling. They follow the tradition of the Prophet that reads, "Should anyone insult or provoke you, or act ignorantly toward you, respond to it by saying, 'I am fasting.'"[106]

This psychological state of peace and tranquility may be a result of a balance in the blood sugar, which may also be a result of the hypoglycemia that is brought about by fasting. Making the intention to refrain from carnal desires and everything that is evil may also be influential in ensuring such a state of mind.[107]

The twenty rakat-prayer, tarawih, in addition to the nightly prayers must also have positive effects upon the spiritual and material world of the person fasting. Both fasting and the prayers observed during Ramadan have uncountable benefits pertaining to this world and to the Hereafter. Yet, believers do not perform daily prayers or observe fasting just because they are beneficial. They try to enjoy the pleasure of Allah and in return Allah rewards them by providing them with a healthy and

[106] Bukhari, Sawm, p. 8.

[107] Gavrankapetanovic F.: Medical aspects of fasting. Med Arh, 51: 25-27, 1997.

peaceful life, which is also a sign of the pleasure and blessing of Allah. Reciting the Qur'an by heart brings about a sense of peace in the heart and mind. It also strengthens the memory. Therefore, in addition to medication some physicians recommend that their Muslim patients fast.[108]

Healthy Muslims do not need to worry about becoming weak and feeble because of fasting. On the contrary, fasting makes them healthier, stronger and gives them more endurance.

In another study, it has been asserted that most of the patients fasting that suffered from ailments such as irritable bowel syndrome and constipation found relief as a result of fasting during Ramadan.[109]

## How does hunger accomplish what abundance cannot?

First of all, it should be made known that staying hungry and fasting are different things. Nevertheless, those who fast gain the benefits of staying hungry, as well. Here, we will investigate the benefits of staying hungry:

---

[108] Attar S: Medical Benefits of Ramadan. International J of Ramadan Fasting Research, 1/1-3, 1997.

[109] Afifi, Z.E.M.: Daily practices, study performance and health during the Ramadan fast. J of Royal Society for Health, 117 (4): 231-5, 1997.

- People who endure hunger gain a deep foresight and perception. They begin to think and comprehend more easily. Contemplation is one half of worship, but eating little is as important as the most precious act of worship. Excessive eating decreases intellectual powers and atrophies the brain.
- Hunger brings about refinement and elegance in the heart.
- Desires are weakened by fasting and the carnal soul becomes obedient. Excessive eating causes obliviousness. It is as difficult to restrain an overfed soul as it is to bridle a wild horse. It is easier to train the soul through fasting. The heart must be enlivened and revived through fasting.
- Those whose stomachs find it easier to be full are hardhearted and merciless. They cannot understand those who suffer from hunger. The heart should not be made hard and pitiless by over eating.
- People who can control their anger are usually peaceful. Hunger restrains the anger and the desire to commit sins and hence acts as an impediment to bad deeds. Enduring hunger and thirst is a struggle (jihad) fought against the carnal soul.
- People who overeat sleep a lot, as well. They spend their life in sleep and this is a threat for the ben-

efits that pertain to both this world and the Hereafter. Hunger makes the nerves alive and active, whereas over-eating makes reading, comprehension and retention difficult.

- It is harmful to overeat and to be overweight. Allah's Messenger is reported to have said to a man who was overweight, "It would be better if this paunch was somewhere else."
- It is better to excel in the art of eating and drinking than in the science of learning how to worship. If we have a healthy body, we will lead a more comfortable life and serve the cause of Allah more. Thus, we may receive blessings in both this world and the Hereafter. Happiness in both worlds can be secured by not becoming a slave of worldly desires. We should not eat if we do not feel hungry and we should leave the table before becoming fully satisfied. Both science and good deeds are based on eating little, the purity of heart is based on sleeping little, and wisdom is based on talking little.
- Eating little is the art of moderation, whereas overeating is an illness. Overeating is a source of sloth; hence those who eat too much cannot achieve their goals.
- Eating little is a fruitful tree and a medicine for a diseased heart. It impedes carnal desires and relieves

the heart. It opens the secret doors to wisdom and brings about eloquence of speech. Overeating is a sign of a lack of wisdom and intelligence. Gluttony is the enemy of the body and a source of regret.

- Eating little is a source of purity and cleanliness for people. Those who eat too much tend to be more forgetful.
- If a person thinks of nothing but food then they are a slave of their carnal soul. This kind of slavery is an obstacle for consciousness. The heart of a gluttonous man is like the grave. Eating little is the first step taken to reach Allah.

## What are the effects of fasting on the human body?

The most important effects of fasting on the human body can be categorized according to various bodily systems:

1. Digestive system
2. Circulatory system
3. Cells
4. Nervous system

### 1. Digestive system

The digestive system, which is comprised of the mouth, salivary glands, tongue, the pharynx, esophagus, stomach, duodenum, liver, and the pancreas functions like a complex computer. This automatic system can easily be worn out as a result of functioning non-stop for 24 hours, nervousness and unhealthy nutrition.

The digestive system of those who fast in Ramadan allows the body to rest for one month a year. The most miraculous effect that fasting has is on the liver. The liver has 15 different tasks in addition to digestion. The liver can become tired and bile secretion may cause the liver to neglect other functions and tasks.

The liver rests for 4 to 6 hours during the fast. Other kinds of diets do not give the liver a chance to rest. Even ten-gram of something is enough to stimulate the liver into functioning. Therefore, fasting is an irreplaceable aide to the liver.

Another positive effect of fasting upon the liver is through blood chemistry. Balancing the nutrients taken into the system and those that are burned is one of the most important tasks of the liver. In Ramadan, when no nutrients are taken in during the day, the liver becomes more efficient in storing nutrients. When it is not busy with storing nutrients it produces globins. As a result, the immune system of the body is strengthened.

The effects of fasting upon the stomach are absolutely positive. All kinds of secretion by the stomach are accustomed according to the amount of food intake. Although there is an accumulation of secretion as a result of hunger, acid secretion stops and thus there is no accumulation of secretion in the stomach while fasting. Making the intention for the fast is a command for the stomach to stop acid secretion. Stomach muscles and secretion cells relax during Ramadan. The stomach, which rests during the day, becomes more efficient in the evening when the fast is broken.

The intestines rest during the fast, as well. This is a result of the decrease in the amount of secretion and work in the intestines. There are Payer's Parches which are an important part of the protective system of the body, under the inner skin of the intestines. During Ramadan, these parches undergo a complete revision and repair. Thus, the body becomes more resistant against ailments that may occur in the digestive system.

## 2. Circulatory system

The blood volume decreases during the fast which in turn relaxes the heart. Moreover, a decrease in the amount of water between the cells reduces the tissue pressure. The pressure in the tissues, which is known as the diastolic blood pressure, is low throughout Ramadan and hence the heart is relaxed.

One of the most important effects of fasting is observed in the blood vessels. Any nutrients that are not sufficiently consumed in the body block and put a strain in the blood vessels. Yet, all the nutrients are completely consumed especially towards the end of the day of fasting.

Kidneys are also a part of the circulatory system. They, too, rest and become healthier during a fast. Fasting helps them to function more efficiently.

## 3. Cells

Establishing a balance in the fluid between the cells and the fluid inside the cells, which is one of the most important physical tasks that influence the cells, becomes easier during the fast and the cells begin to function more efficiently. The epithelial cells, which are responsible for continuous secretion, are relieved during the fast and thus they begin to function more efficiently.

## 4. Nervous system

Both ablution and fasting have a positive effect upon the nervous system. The inner glands in the nervous system become relieved after taking ablution or observing fast. When a believer makes the intention to worship Allah, the idea of worshipping Allah and the pleasure it gives relieve the nervous system, as well. Hence, it begins to function more efficiently.

Blood anabolism: It is known that there is reflex that stimulates the bone marrow to produce more blood whenever there is a need in the body. The bone marrow is where the blood is produced. During the fast, the amount of nutrients in the blood is at its lowest degrees and this stimulates the bone marrow to produce blood. As the liver is able to be at rest during the fast, it produces the substances the bone marrow needs for blood production more easily.

As a result of the miraculous wisdom behind fasting those people who are fasting that are underweight and weak are able to put on weight, while those who are overweight lose weight. This is a result of the balancing mechanism initiated by fasting.

The verse . . . And it is better for you that you fast, if you only knew (al-Baqarah 2:184) reminds us how much we should be thankful to Allah for His blessings.[110]

## Can diabetics observe the fast of Ramadan?

Many diabetics observe the fast during Ramadan without any hesitation or without any thought about their illness. Medical specialists who are aware of fasting as a religious obligation may find it difficult to decide whether diabetics should fast or not. Fasting may endanger their life and the sugar rate in the blood may decrease drastically, causing hypoglycemia. Hypoglycemia can cause some other complications as well.

On the other hand, it cannot be denied that fasting gives a spiritual pleasure and sooths the patient as it is

[110] Nurbaki, Haluk, «Kur›an-ı Kerim›den Ayetler ve İlmi Gerçekler»

mandated by Allah.[111] It is a well-known fact that stress increases the blood sugar by increasing the secretion of catecholamine. Anything that may decrease stress and discomfort, for instance, the peace of mind fasting provides is effective in controlling the blood sugar. Thus, fasting may have benefits for even the sufferers of diabetes.

## Are all diabetics exempt from fasting?

The diabetics that have the following characteristics can fast in the month of Ramadan:[112]

1. Male diabetics that are above twenty can observe fast. That is, the type of diabetes from which adults and the elderly suffer is not an impediment for fasting.
2. Pregnant and nursing mothers above twenty who are diabetic should not observe fasting.
3. Diabetics who want to fast should have a normal weight or slightly over average.
4. There must be no serious variations in the amount of blood sugar and no hypoglycemia, no ketoses, and no infection.

---

[111] Athar S.: Health Concerns for Believers Contemporary Issues.

[112] Athar S, Habib M.: Management of Stable Type 2 Diabetes Mellitus (NIDMM) During Islamic Fasting in Ramadan. Proceedings of the First International Congress on Health and Ramadan. p. 203, Casablanca, 1994.

5. The diabetic should not have another serious illness such as hypertension (200/120 mm Hg), rheumatoid arthritis, kidney stones, chronic obstructive pulmonary disease, etc. if they are to fast.
6. The body of the diabetic must be responsive to diets prescribed by doctors.
7. The body of the diabetic must respond to medical treatment if the patient is to be eligible for fasting.

## What is recommended for diabetics observing the fast?

Diabetics who are not insulin-dependent can observe the fast under medical supervision, providing that they keep the following recommendations in mind:

1. Diabetics who want to fast should keep their blood sugar rate at a certain level by maintaining a strict diet and ensuring that they get the proper amount of medicine. For instance, they should try to keep the glucose hemoglobin level at 7 mgr/dlt (100 cm3). The blood sugar rate when hungry should be under 150 mgr/dlt and the regular blood sugar rate should be about 250 mgr/dlt.
2. They can observe one or two days of voluntary fast prior to Ramadan and see the test results before deciding whether to fast or not.

3. They should strictly follow the diets prescribed for them by their doctors and they should refrain from carbohydrates and fats.
4. They should break their fast in the evening by drinking some fruit juice or eating one or two dates.
5. They should find out their blood sugar rate before they break the fast in the evening. They should then take the regular dose of insulin and other medications before having an iftar meal that has controlled calories.
6. They should never neglect the pre-dawn meal.
7. The blood sugar rate should be taken and recorded before the nightly prayers. If it is above 250-mgr/100 cm3, they should make the iftar meal the next day 20 % less.
8. They should have a light meal of about 100 calories after the tarawih prayer when it is time to go to bed.
9. The blood sugar rate should be taken before sahur. If it is above 250-mgr/100 cm3, they should lessen the sahur meal by 20 %. If it is above 350-mgr/100 cm3, they should not go on fasting. The dehydration caused by fasting may lead to diabetic keto-acidoses (increased production of ketones). Diabetics should drink at least two glasses of water before beginning to fast.

10. They should go on performing their regular physical activities and daily tasks while fasting. They should not spend the day in bed. A 10 to 15-minute exercise shortly before the iftar meal may be beneficial.
11. The blood sugar rate should be controlled in case of hypoglycemia. If it goes below 50 mgr/dlt during the fast, the patient must break thefast immediately.
12. Some symptoms of hypoglycemia (a hazardous decrease of blood sugar) are as follows:
    - Over perspiration and trembling
    - Hear palpitation
    - Dizziness and fainting
    - Lack of concentration
    - Nervousness, susceptibility, and anxiety
    - Cold, sticky, and wet skin

## What are the benefits of fasting for the kidney and urinary tract?

In a study carried out at the Faculty of Medicine at al-Azhar University, Cairo, 70 fasters that suffered from kidney stones or urinary tract infections were examined. The urine and blood samples of the people fasting were analyzed both when the subjects were fasting and when they were not. The results of the analyses are as follows:

1. Fasting during Ramadan causes no variance in the amount of calcium, sodium, potassium, uric acid, urea, and creatine in the serum of the fasters that suffer from kidney stones or urinary tract infections.
2. The amount of calcium and uric acid in the urine decreases during the fast. This is a desirable result.
3. There is a significant decrease in the amount of calcium in the urine of those who suffer from urinary tract infections.
4. An increase was observed in the amount of sodium in the urine of patients that suffer from kidney stones. This is very important, for it impedes the formation of stones in the kidney. That is to say, fasting has positive effects upon the process of stone-formation in the kidney. Although this is a very complex process, the abundance of urine is a protective factor. Fasters must drink water abundantly at night or during sahur to compensate for the liquid they cannot take during the day.
5. Patients suffering from pyelonephritis should break the fast at acute periods or when there is extreme renal colic that results in vomiting. It is better to break the fast in such cases and redeem it later.
6. Patients that have difficulty in relieving themselves of urine should not drink too much water.

They should also refrain from eating too much. A good diet is crucial in the last phase of urological diseases.

## Is fasting beneficial for the heart?

The heart pumps up to 80 cm3 of blood at every contraction from the left ventricle to the aorta, which is the main artery of the body. This means that the blood is moving 5.5 liter a minute.

The one-minute discharge volume of the heart increases by 30-40 % after meals. This is a result of the increase in the amount of blood that is used in the digestive system. Such an increase is truly significant, for the amount of blood pumped by the heart to the aorta increases from 5.5 liters to 7 or even 7.5 liters. Certainly this over-work could cause a strain on the heart.

The amount of blood that flows through the vessels is 500 cm3 while resting. After a meal this amount increases by 50 to 300 %. The volume, which is normally 500 cm3 increases to 1 to 1.5 litersa minute after meals. That is the reason why the body becomes tired and sleepy after the meals. The stomach and the vessels need a lot of blood and therefore less blood goes to the brain.

The heart of a person fasting beats more easily, particularly in the afternoons. During the fast it beats about 15,000 times less than the average amount of times on a non-fasting day. The heart is thus relaxed and strengthened through fasting.

This result can only be partly achieved by medicines called beta-blockers. These medicines influence the body in such a way that the heart beats become less frequent even when the body needs more blood. Certainly fasting is a better, more natural and healthier means of balancing the supply and demand. If a person observes fasting regularly and in the way that Allah's Messenger did, they will be spared most heart diseases.

## Should one fast while suffering from heart disease, angina, or asthma?

People who have coronary heart diseases can fast. Fasting is not harmful for such diseases. Beta-blockers, calcium channel blockers and nitrates, which have enduring effects, can be used to help the person fast more easily.

A heart attack is a serious disease that is caused by the clogging or shrinking of one of the coronary arteries which feed the heart muscle, and hence the death of some part of the heart muscle takes place. Heart attacks are preceded by and characterized with chest pains called angina pectoris, which inform the sufferer about the coming attack. A faster can break his fast in case of such severe pains.

Asthma is an illness that occurs as periodic attacks, some symptoms of which are coughing and dyspnea (breathing difficulty). Having asthma is not an excuse for not observing the fast. It is not harmful for those who suffer from asthma. Medications with enduring effects should be used. However, the person should break the fast in case of an asthmatic crisis.[113]

## Is it scientifically valid that fasting is a source for renewal of the body?

Alexis Carrel, who was awarded the Nobel Prize in Medicine in 1940, writes in his book *L'Homme, Cet Inconnu* that during a fast the nutrients stored up in the body are burned, that they are replaced by new nutrients and that this brings about a renewal of the body adding that this process is essential for a healthy body.

The nervous system is relieved and relaxed during the fast. The relief and happiness we get when performing an act of worship erases almost all kind of strain and uneasiness in our heart. Stress, which is one of the most important problems of present times, thus, disappears to a great extent.[114]

---

[113] Özyazıcı, Alpaslan, Din ve Bilimin Iþığında Oruç ve Sağlık, pp. 169-170.

[114] Nurbaki, p. 98.

## Some recommendations concerning health during Ramadan

The sort of food eaten during Ramadan should not be greatly different from that eaten at other times and it should be quite modest. It should be enough so that you can maintain a normal weight. However, fasting is a good opportunity for those who are overweight to get rid of some extra weight.[115]

When observing the fast during the long days of the year, food that is digested slowly, such as fibrous foodstuffs, should be preferred rather than food that is easy to digest. The sort of food in the former group is digested in 8 hours, whereas that of the latter group can be digested in 3 to 4 hours.

Foodstuffs such as barley, wheat, oats, millet, semolina, beans, lentil, flour, rice, etc. are examples of foods that are digested slowly. These cereal grains are complex carbohydrates that are rich in nutrients.

Foodstuffs that contain sugar and white flour are foods that are burned fast. These are refined and purified carbohydrates. Fibrous foodstuffs are also difficult to digest. Foodstuffs with bran such as wheat flour, grains, and seeds, vegetables such as green beans, peas, spinach,

[115] Haffejee F: Some Health Guidelines for Ramadan. Proceedings of the Second International Congress on 'Health and Ramadan', p. 86, Istanbul, 1997.

parsley, Swiss chard and peppers, dried fruit, such as apricots, figs, prunes as well as almonds are some of fibrous foodstuffs.

## Is it harmful to consume fried foods during Ramadan? What about smoking?

People who are fasting should refrain from fried food as much as possible. Fried foods are unhealthy and should be restricted during Ramadan. Such food causes indigestion, stomach acid, sourness in the throat, and weight problems. However, foodstuffs such as fruits, vegetables, meat, chicken, fish, bread, and milk products should all be included in Ramadan meals, ensuring a healthy and well-balanced diet.

As mentioned before, fried and fatty food should be avoided. Desserts which are too sweet should not be eaten nor should too much tea be consumed at sahur, for too much tea causes accumulation of urine. Discharging too much urine leads to loss of many mineral salts, which are beneficial to the body. Sahur should be a light meal.

Smokers should begin to reduce how much they smoke a few weeks before Ramadan. Everybody knows that smoking is harmful to the body and that it is not something that is desirable. Therefore, the month of Ramadan is a time to reduce or even stop smoking. A little effort and patience will suffice to give up smoking in

Ramadan. Actually, many addicts have been known to completely give up smoking in Ramadan.

## What to eat at the *iftar* and *sahur* meals?

At sahur, food made with flour should be chosen so as to help last through the day. Meat is a perfect source of proteins and is digested slowly. Those who find it difficult to endure hunger should eat something made with meat at sahur.

Dates can be eaten especially at iftar, for they are a perfect source of sugar, fiber, carbohydrate, potassium, and magnesium.

Almonds contain little fat and they are rich in proteins and fiber. Bananas are good sources of potassium, magnesium, and carbohydrate.

From iftar until bedtime the person fasting should have a large intake of water, fruit juice, and fruits. This will help them to maintain the desirable liquid level in the body.

## What to do in case of trivial ailments?

Constipation: Constipation is an ailment that can be caused by hemorrhoids or fissures and gives one a sense of bloating. Eating overly refined food, not drinking enough water or fruit juice and not eating enough fibrous food are some of the elements that can cause constipation.

The remedy is to drink a lot of water, to stay away from refined foods, to eat whole wheat, whole fiber bread and to choose fibrous foods over refined foods.

Indigestion and gas: Eating too much fried or fatty food, preferring gas-producing foods such as spicy food, eggs, cabbages, or pulses and drinking carbonated acid drinks are among the things that cause indigestion and gas.

People that suffer from indigestion and gas should eat less, abstain from eating fried and gas-producing foods, and drink a lot of water or fruit juice.

Lethargy and hypotension (low blood pressure): Among the symptoms of hypotension are over perspiration, weakness, fatigue, energy loss, dizziness, a pale countenance and lethargy. Low blood pressure can result in the loss of consciousness. The person fasting should be cautious, since fasting (especially in the afternoon) may cause lethargy and hypotension.

Having a lower intake of liquid and hence a decrease in the amount of salt in the body may bring about such a state. In such a case, the person fasting should rest in a cool place and be sure to have ample liquid and salt at sahur and iftar. For example, they can drink some salty liquid. When the above-mentioned symptoms occur, the blood pressure should be taken with a sphygmomanometer in order to see whether the blood pressure is low or not. If it is very low, the person fasting must break the fast. People who have high blood pressure should consult their doctor to rearrange the timing of their medications and to adjust these to the time of the sahur and iftar meals.

Headaches: Especially coffee and cigarette addicts will have frequent headaches in the first few days of Ramadan. These headaches are usually accompanied by a sense sleeplessness and hunger. Headaches during the day are not generally severe. However, those that may occur about the end of the fasting day and toward iftar can at times be quite serious and may come about as a result of hypotension. Such headaches may cause nausea before iftar.

It is recommended that people who have such headaches during Ramadan start to decrease the amount of the coffee they drink and of the amount of cigarettes they smoke a few weeks before Ramadan. Non-caffeine drinks such as herb tea or normal tea can replace coffee. Going to bed early and getting a good night's sleep or having a nap during the day may also help to relieve the headaches.

Hypoglycemia (deficiency of sugar in the blood): Weakness, dizziness, fatigue, low concentration, frequent perspiration, tremors, palpitations, headaches and difficulty in carrying out physical activities are some of the symptoms for hypoglycemia.

Eating refined carbohydrates and too much sugar at sahur is the main cause of such a condition during Ramadan. The body secretes a great deal of insulin in response to the refined carbohydrates and sugar and this causes hypoglycemia.

People that have hypoglycemia are advised to take a small and limited amount of food or drink that contains sugar. Diabetics should consult their doctor for relevant medications and applications during Ramadan.

Muscle cramps: The main cause for muscle cramps is a lack of calcium, magnesium and potassium in the body. Fasters are recommended to eat vegetables, fruits, milk and milk products, meat and dates, all of which contain these minerals in abundance, at sahur and iftar.

Peptic ulcers, gastroenteritis, gastritis, and hiatus hernia: These ailments may become more severe during Ramadan. They may produce a sense of burning under the rib cage inside the stomach, which can reach as far as to the throat. Spicy foods, coffee, and cola may worsen these illnesses.

The acid level of the stomach can be controlled with a correct medical treatment. Those who suffer from peptic ulcers and hiatus hernias must consult their doctor before deciding to fast in Ramadan.

Kidney stones: One of the causes of kidney stones is a lack of a sufficient amount of water in the body. People that suffer from kidney stones or those whose kidneys are apt to form stones must drink a lot of water during iftar and sahur.

Rheumatism: In Ramadan believers perform 20-rakat tarawih prayer after the 13-rakat obligatory night prayer, which makes a total of 33 rakats. This is not too much for healthy people. On the contrary, these long prayers serve as an exercise that is absolutely beneficial for the body especially after eating a heavy iftar meal. However, the elderly and those who suffer from rheumatism (pain and inflammation in the joints) may find it quite difficult and painful to observe such long prayers.

People who cannot bend their knees or ankles are allowed to perform prayers in a sitting position. Allah the Almighty does not command people to do anything that they cannot do.[116] He says, Allah intends every facility for you; He does not want to put you in difficulties (al-Baqarah 2:185).

[116] Özyazıcı, pp. 173-176.

# Chapter 7
# Some Questions and Answers

## Is it right to observe the fast without any interruption for three consequent months during Rajab, Sha'ban, and Ramadan?

The only time allocated to fasting in Islam is the month of Ramadan. That is, the fast of Ramadan is obligatory, but there is no obligatory fast in the month of Rajab or Sha'ban. Muslims can fast many days of Rajab and Sha'ban, but it is a bid'ah (undesirable innovation) to spend the whole month fasting. Mother Aisha reported that the Prophet never completed the fasting of any other month than that of Ramadan and that he never fasted the greater part of a month, except that of Sha'ban.[117]

Some people observe the fast for three subsequent months during Rajab, Sha'ban, and Ramadan for seven

[117] Muslim, Siyam, 175, 176.

years, and then sacrifice cattle. There is no such worship in Islam and certainly it is a bid'ah.

The life of Allah's Messenger is a perfect example for believers, for he led a life that is in line with the purpose of creation and the nature of humanity. Although he wanted to worship more, he arranged the time and amount that he worshipped in such a way that even the feeblest person could perform the same. He even prevented those who wanted to worship more, saying: "I am the most God-fearing, the one nearest to Allah among you; I sometimes perform prayers and sometimes sleep; I sometimes observe fast and sometimes do not."[118] He was a man of perfect balance and moderation. Sometimes he fasted for days and nights non-stop, without a break (wisaal). However, when his companions wanted to follow his example he prevented them, saying that Allah nourished him with food and drink. Moderation must be a principle for believers in any kind of worship. Those who want to fast more than what is obligatory are recommended by Prophet Muhammad to follow the example of Prophet David. Prophet David used to fast every other day.[119] Muslims are not allowed to fast more than this.

---

[118] Bukhari, Nikah, 1.

[119] Muslim, Siyam, 189.

## Is there a ten-day fast before the Eid-al Adha (Festivity of Sacrifice) for Muslims?

It is not evident in any of the authentic traditions that Allah's Messenger observed such a fast. There is only a weak tradition reported by mother Hafsa that reads: "There are four things that the Messenger of Allah never neglected: Observing the fast on the day of Ashura, the first ten days of Dhu al-Hijja, and three days every month, and offering fajr sunna prayers early in the morning."[120] There are authentic traditions that point to the three practices of the Prophet mentioned in this tradition except that of the fast on the first ten days of Dhu al-Hijja. On the contrary, Abu Hurayra reported that "Allah's Messenger prohibited fasting on the Day of Arafat."[121] Some scholars are of the opinion that this prohibition is only for pilgrims, since the Prophet did not want the pilgrims to be feeble and exhausted while performing the pilgrimage. They argue that it is better for people who are not pilgrims to fast and point to the following tradition as evidence: "Fasting on the day of Arafat absolves the sins for two years: the previous year and the coming year."[122]

To conclude, there is no proof for fasting on the first ten days of Dhu al-Hijja in the authentic traditions. There-

[120] Ahmad ibn Hanbal, Musnad, 6/287; Nasai, Siyam, 83.

[121] Ahmad ibn Hanbal, Musnad, 6/287.

[122] Muslim, Siyam, 197.

fore, even if it is good and rewarding to observe this, it is not possible to say whether this fast is obligatory or sunna.

## Can those who fast use *siwak* to cleanse their teeth during the period of fasting?

Highly esteemed scholars of Islamic jurisprudence have fervently advised Muslims to avoid anything that may harm or invalidate fasting. Although siwak, a piece of the root of the arak tree used as a toothbrush, and even though it is highly valued and recommended in Islam, it is better not to use it during the fast, for there is a possibility that the juice of siwak or saliva may reach the throat while cleaning the teeth, and thus invalidate the fast. Some scholars have asserted that it can be used until noon, but not in the afternoon. Still others have claimed that it can be used anytime, provided it is dry when used during the fast.[123] Yet, no matter when or how it is used, it is probable that the siwak will harm the fast and break it. Therefore, it is better not to use it.

## What is the Prophet's practice concerning eating?

Allah's Messenger is the best example for us in every aspect. The way he ate his meals and the amount he ate

[123] Zuhayli, 2/637; Ibn Kudama, al-Mugni, 1/110.

for each meal are also perfect practices that should be followed by believers.

The Messenger refrained from over-eating throughout his life. Actually, he used to eat less than what his body desired or than what he could eat. Mother Aisha said, "The Messenger of Allah did not satisfy his hunger for three consecutive days. He could have if he had wanted to. However, he preferred staying hungry and feeding the poor."[124]

Abu Karima reported: "I heard the following from the Messenger of Allah. He said, 'The children of Adam will never fill a container that is worse or more evil than his stomach. It will suffice him to fill it with some morsels of food that will keep him on his feet, otherwise, he should divide his stomach into three parts: one third for his food, the other for his drink and the other third for his breath."[125]

Obviously Allah's Messenger advised eating less and he contented himself by eating less. It is evident in other traditions that he used to eat twice a day, once in the morning and once in the evening and that he used to leave the dining table without having fully satisfied his hunger.[126]

---

[124] Ibn Maja, At'ima, 48.

[125] Ibn Maja, At'ima, 50.

[126] Canan, Ibrahim, Hz. Peygamber'in Sunnetinde Terbiye, (Education in the Teachings of the Prophet) p. 218-220.

Inspired by the Prophet's advice, scholars have all pointed out that over-eating is harmful to the body. For instance, Ibn Sina (Avicenna) said: "Every illness is caused by what is eaten or drunk." Imam Ghazali said: "The stomach is the place where ailments and calamities are born and increase." Some scholars say that Allah the Almighty has summarized the science of medicine in the following part of the verse: Eat and drink, but do not waste by over-eating or consuming in unnecessary ways; assuredly, He does not love the wasteful (A'raf 7:31).

Finally, how one should eat in a way that is parallel to the Prophet's example can be summarized as follows:

1. Do not eat unless you are really hungry.
2. Stop eating before you are fully satisfied.

An interpretation of the above verse by the renowned scientist and physician Ibn Sina reads as follows: "I will summarize the science of medicine in a couple of words, for the eloquence of speech lies in its brevity: Do not eat too much when you eat. Do not eat again until four or five hours have passed after your last meal. Good digestion is the source of healing. That is, eat as much as you can easily digest. Having another meal without waiting long enough after the last meal is the most exhausting factor for the stomach and the body."[127]

[127] Nursi, vol. 1, p. 661.

It is clear that if we follow the example of Allah's Messenger and imitate his eating habits, we will most likely lead a healthy life and will be able to avoid problems such as obesity.

However, a tradition about the amount of lawful food is to be noted here that Allah's Messenger says: "Allah will not question His servants on three things:

1) The things they eat or drink at sahur.
2) The things they eat or drink at iftar.
3) The things a person eats with his brothers-in-religion."[128]

## How can the breath of a person fasting be thought to be sweeter than musk?

The unpleasant breath of a person fasting is a result of that fast. Therefore, it is the means of a reward that is sweeter and more pleasant than musk and amber in the Hereafter. It is to be noted that angels enjoy such sweet fragrances of roses, flowers, musk, and amber. Sweet odors are like keys that open secret treasures in the world of meaning, and certainly the odor of the breath of the one who is fasting is one of these odors.

It should also be noted that unpleasant breath occurs because of hunger, especially during the long days of sum-

---

[128] Ayni, Umdat al-Qari, 10/302.

mer. But before Allah this odor is sweeter than musk, a scent that is thought to be the sweetest fragrance. Nevertheless, it should be made clear that this fact about the breath of a person fasting should not prevent them from cleansing their teeth by using a siwak or toothbrush.

## Some people eat openly during Ramadan, saying "what is known by Allah cannot be concealed from his servants." Is this not a major sin?

Committing a sin, no matter whether it is open or hidden is prohibited. Yet, whoever yields to Satan or their carnal soul and commits a sin must conceal their sin. Concealing a sin is beneficial for the following reasons:

1. A person who commits a sin should be pleased if his sin is not discovered by other people. Allah the Almighty does not like human beings to commit sins openly. Also Allah's Messenger said, "Whosoever covers his sin in the world, Allah will hide that sin from His servants in the Hereafter."

2. It is obviously not pleasant to commit sins openly. But Allah may forgive those who are repentant and who hide their sins. Allah's Messenger said: "Whosoever happens to commit a sin must conceal it! He must keep the covering of Allah over it!"

3. People who commit sins should be embarrassed in front of human beings. They should hide their sins at

least, so as to prevent people gossiping about them. Do not forget that feeling ashamed because of a bad thing is a good and favorable deed. There is no religion for shameless people.

4. It is also necessary to conceal a sin so as not to be a bad example and to encourage others to commit sins. Therefore, a sinner must conceal their sins, and more importantly, must try hard not to commit sins even in secret. Sins are like deadly poison. People who have a sincere faith are afraid of committing sins. The Prophet says: "A believer feels his sin to be like a mountain and is afraid of falling down it. But a hypocrite thinks that his sin is like a fly on his nose that will soon fly away."

## Some people say "those who do not perform daily prayers or are not careful with their other religious duties should not fast in vain." Is it not possible, then, for a sinner to worship?

Some people follow the motto "Everything or nothing!" and argue, "We should either fulfill all of the decrees of the religion or none of them." This is not true, for it is a general principle of Islam not to give up the partial practice of any worship that cannot be performed in its completeness. A person who has committed a few sins should not think that they are ruined and therefore go on committing other sins. A sinner who observes the fast may not get the great reward for the fast, but they will not be questioned about fasting in the Hereafter, either. They will be seen as having paid their debt concerning the obligatory fast. Moreover, they may even find a way to escape the bonds of their sins because of their fasting.

The more one diminishes committing sin the better. Giving up a sin in fear of Allah is a sign of faith. If a sinner observes fasting or paying the zakat, we should say: "At least do not give up on these good deeds." If they were to give up these, they may become more alienated to the religion. We should herald good tidings to people rather than threatening them and leaving them in complete despair. Allah's Messenger cursed those who made people hate religion by causing them to lose hope and faith in the infinite mercy and compassion of Allah. We should facilitate and ease religion, rather than making it difficult.

Imam Rabbani says, "It is a great blessing to repent for and avoid all sins. If you cannot do this, it is also a blessing to refrain from some of your sins. This may help you to get rid of all other sins. If you cannot get hold of something completely, it is advisable to take hold of as much as you can."[129]

Even though performing daily prayers is the most important worship in Islam, it would not be correct or wise to tell someone who does not perform their prayers

[129] Imam Rabbani, Maktubat Rabbani, vol. II, letter 66.

not to fast. On the contrary, one should recommend such a person not to commit greater sin of giving up the worship of fasting.

It is reported that a young man told the Prophet that he could not give up three sins of telling lies, adultery, and taking alcohol. Allah's Messenger said: "Of these three sins, for me abandon telling lies." The man agreed and left. Later, he thought, "If I go on committing the other two sins and tell the Prophet when I meet him that I have not done so, I will be telling a lie. If I tell him that I have gone on committing them, he will make me bear the consequence of committing those sins." Thus, he gave up committing the other two sins, as well. As we can see, abandoning one sin can often lead to abandoning other sins as well.

Moreover, it would not be correct or wise to tell someone who does not perform their prayers not to fast because daily prayers are the most important worship and thus are of the highest priority to perform. On the contrary, one should recommend such a person not to commit greater sin of abandoning the worship of fasting thinking in despair that they committed the great sin of not performing daily prayers.

Anybody who declares the words of Shahada and accepts these words in their heart is a Muslim. People who commit sins are not exempted from Islam. It is also a known fact that anyone who never associated partners with Allah recognizing His Oneness will go to Paradise in the end after being punished for their sins.

Certainly, these glad tidings should not encourage people to commit sins. Each sin leaves a black spot on the heart. From each sin there is a way towards unbelief, which may cause the sinner to stay in Hell forever. Allah's wrath is concealed in sins. Therefore, we should refrain from all kinds of sin.

## Is it true that it is possible to eat "until a white thread is distinguishable from a black one" before the fast begins?

The word "streak" as so often been interpreted as "thread" in the verse ...And you can eat and drink until you discern the white streak of dawn against the blackness of night (al-Baqarah 2:187) is the equivalent for the Arabic word hayt, which is the beginning of the dawn. The white streak is that of daytime and the blackness is the darkness of the night.

A man who heard this verse said to the Prophet: "I took two threads, one black and the other white, and kept them under my pillow and went on looking at them throughout the night but could not make anything out of it." Allah's Messenger explained to him, "That verse means the darkness of the night and the whiteness of the dawn."

## If one has a tooth extracted, does this invalidate the fast?

The extraction of a tooth or teeth does not invalidate the fast. But if a person is given an injection before the tooth is pulled out, the fast is invalidated. If one swallows blood when the tooth is extracted, this also invalidates the fast. However, this requires that a day be made up and not a sixty-day expiation.

## Do sins such as telling lies, backbiting, and looking at the unlawful invalidate the fast?

Although it is stated in a tradition that backbiting, gossip, false oaths, and lustful looks at the unlawful invalidate the fast, Imam Azam explained this tradition, saying, "These sins harm the reward of the fast, and not the essence of the fast. Such fasting is reprehensible, but not invalid." That is, although the person who commits such sins is saved from the obligation of fasting, they will not get the great reward for the fast. Remember that Allah's Messenger said: "Many an observer of the fast will not receive any reward from his fasting but the pain of hunger and thirst."[130]

Fasting is a blessing and trust for believers. They must comply with and protect the rules of fasting that has been put in their trust so as not to let them erode and disappear.

[130] Ahmad ibn Hanbal, Musnad, 2/441; Darimi, Riqaq, 12.

Refraining from looking lustfully at the unlawful is very important in Islam and believers must be very careful about this matter. Concerning such unlawful looks Allah's Messenger says, "The unlawful look is one of the poisonous arrows of the cursed Satan. Whoever gives that up for fear of Allah, Allah will reward those servants of His with a faith, the sweetness of which they will feel in their heart."[131]

In addition to this, those who fast must also protect their tongue. The Prophet said: "Fasting is a shield against fire. It protects unless it is smashed by backbiting. The person fasting must not act ignorantly and indulge in obscene talk. Should anyone insult him, he must say, 'I am fasting.'"[132] Speech does not invalidate fasting. But silence, contemplation, and remembrance of Allah are more suitable and desirable, for they help the believer win their fight against their carnal self.

We must also protect our ears against sins just as we protect our eyes and tongue. Just as talking obscenely is forbidden, listening to such talk is also forbidden. Our other limbs, such as hands and feet, must also be protected against sins. A person who is fasting that commits sins is like an ill person who drinks poison instead of medicine; for sins are like poison. They nullify the rewards of

[131] Hakim, Mustadrak, 4/349.

[132] Bukhari, Sawm, 9; Nasai, Siyam, 42; Ahmad ibn Hanbal, 2/273.

worship. Therefore, we must not destroy the rewards of our worship by committing sins.

## Do things such as face cream, lipstick, eye or nose drops, liniments, vaccinations, chewing gum, tooth paste and scents invalidate the fast?

Creams do not invalidate fasting, but injections do. Eye drops do not harm fasting. Donating blood does not, either.

If medicine applied to the nose is liquid, it nullifies the fast, but if it is solid, it does not.

Hair gel and deodorants do not invalidate fasting.

Lipstick does not harm fasting. But if it is swallowed, the fast is nullified. Those who habitually receive the taste of lipstick in their mouths should not use lipstick while fasting.

When giving blood at the hospital, sometimes some alcohol is applied to the arm before and after the syringe is injected. This does not affect the fast.

Ear drops invalidate fasting, whereas eye drops do not.

Vaccinations done by scratching the skin do not nullify fasting, either.

Rubbing a liniment or some other lotion to the body does not invalidate fasting.

It is not proper for a person fasting to chew gum. Even though it is said to be not prohibited, it is better not to chew it.

It is improper to brush the teeth using toothpaste. Teeth can be cleansed without using toothpaste. But it is better not to do this in case water flows into the throat. Even if using toothpaste does not invalidate the fast, it is unadvisable because of the risk of swallowing it. If it is swallowed or if it goes into the throat, the fast is nullified and requires a make-up day.

Using birth control medications to delay menstruation so as to be able to fast is not prohibited, but it is not necessary, either.

Smelling musk, roses, or rose water is not prohibited. Smelling flowers and scents does not harm the fast, either. Perfumes that are not natural are said to be improper to use during the fast.

## How can we make the best of the blessed times such as the month of Ramadan?

In a tradition Allah's Messenger says: "My community will not be despised so long as it revives and passes the month of Ramadan with worship." The exact word used in the original wording of the tradition is ihya, meaning "reviving," "restoring to vigor," and "evaluating in the best way." Then, how can it be revived and restored to life? That is, how can we breathe new life into a "dead time"?

Allah the Almighty has ornamented the year with special and magnificent stations of blessing in which His servants can reform and purify their souls. They should call at these stations, which are special days for worship and supplication to Allah, and enliven themselves with fasting, prayers, charities, and the recitation of the Qur'an. Only thus can they be saved from the attribute "despised" that occurs in the tradition above to warn the believers.

The only way to make the best use of such blessed times is to devote the nights and days to worship and remembrance (dhikr) of Allah. Then, the nights of believers are as illuminated as their daytimes. Thus, the day does not end with the night prayers ('isha) or the voluntary 20-rakat tarawih prayers in Ramadan. The nights of believers sparkle with voluntary nightly prayers, supplications, remembrance, and glorification of Allah, and the sincere pleading for forgiveness (tawba), for they know that these are the most precious times when supplications are accepted and answered by Allah. The predawn meal becomes a real feast for every member of the family, since even those who are not eligible to fast wake up and join the meal.

The following recommendations should be kept in mind so as to revive and utilize Ramadan and its blessed nights:

1. In Ramadan, believers should try to perform their prayers in congregation at the mosque if possible and if they are healthy. Thus, they will get more rewards for their prayers and also they will be able to meet friends, neighbors, and other believers at such blessed times.

2. Whenever believers go to the mosque, it is recommended that they take their adolescent children with them, for this is very important in the formation of their religious thought. The youth may comprehend the importance of congregation, solidarity, and cooperation better and more easily at such occasions

3. On the holy days and nights of Ramadan, believers should try to find out means of congratulating their relatives, neighbors, and friends. Believers should concern themselves with worries and troubles of other people and offer help. They should also delight in their joy and happiness.

4. On such days and nights believers are advised to recite and listen to the Qur'an as much as possible, attend conversations and lessons about the Qur'an and the traditions of the Prophet and listen to preaching and sermons, for a religious and spiritual atmosphere will give them peace. In particular, contemplating the meaning of the verses of the Qur'an and the prophetic

traditions will help believers to improve their Islamic knowledge.

5. Remembrance and glorification of Allah the Almighty, asking for His forgiveness and supplicating for His mercy and blessings will strengthen the sense of servitude to Allah.

6. Prayers on holy days and nights will help believers attain Allah's pleasure more easily, for the moment a servant is closest to Allah is the time when they perform their prayers. Prayers are the best means for remembrance of Allah. Believers should worship on such days and nights with utmost care.

7. On such days and nights believers should prostrate before Allah and beg Him for peace and solidarity and protection all the Muslims and other people on the Earth from every kind of disaster. This will give the person the sense and feeling that they are a worthy member of humanity.

8. And finally, at such times believers should scrutinize their servitude to Allah and try to erase their defects, which is a task to be carried out all the time but with more care in Ramadan. They should focus on what role they play and how beneficent they are to the society as a grandparent, a son, a daughter, a businessman, a teacher, a student, a manager, or a citizen. On the holy days and nights of Ramadan every believer should detect their faults and deficiencies through self-criticism and

have the hope and determination to be more beneficent, more successful, and more productive.

## Can women use medication to delay their menstruation in Ramadan?

There is no religious objection to delaying menstruation by using medicine in order to fast, recite the Qur'an, and perform other acts of worship during Ramadan. In fact, there was such a practice of delaying menstruation during the lifetime of Allah's Messenger. At that time women used to drink araq water to delay their periods. Abdullah ibn Umar says that there is no fault in using this water. Today, various medications do exist to delay menstruation. However, medical experts do not recommend delaying it, since such a practice may cause some health problems.

In short, women can take medicine to delay menstruation and fast in Ramadan if they want, but it is better not to do so if there is a risk for their health and if their periods are not regular.

## Should people act as if they are fasting even if they are not?

Travelers whose journey end after the time when the fast begins must behave as if they are fasting and they must not eat, drink, or have sexual intercourse.

This is the same for somebody who recovers from an illness during the day. They must act as if they are fasting, as well. According to some scholars this is incumbent on them, while others say it is not incumbent, but virtuous.

Travelers, patients, or women who are menstruating or have post child birth bleeding do not have to act as if they are fasting. They can eat and drink. Nevertheless, it is more polite to do so in secret so as not to cause people who do not know about their excuse to think badly of them.

## Is fasting invalidated if someone puts medicine or something like a clove on an aching tooth?

Putting something like a clove on an aching tooth and feeling its bitterness or taste in the throat does not invalidate the fast. Yet, if the person were to swallow some part of it, then the fast is invalidated. It is stated in some sources (like the book Muhit), "The taste or odor of medicine does not invalidate the fast." In some other books of canonical jurisprudence there is the judgment that "Swallowing unintentionally a morsel of food smaller than a chickpea, which remained between the teeth, does not nullify the fast."

Nevertheless, if possible believers must be cautious and take their medicine after iftar and at night until sahur.

In case of any emergency concerning health believers are, without any doubt, allowed to break their fast. Urgent situations such as unbearable pain make those things that are reprehensible permissible.

## What should the elderly who are feeble and have no possibility to fast do?

People who are not able to fast must pay compensation to the poor and needy for each of the fasts they miss. The amount of this expiatory payment is equal to the amount of the charity of fast breaking. Money can be given instead of foodstuffs, such as wheat and dates. If a person who cannot fast gives a poor person enough money to live on for one day for each of the days missed, then they are freed from the responsibility to fast.

However, if a person who does not fast because of an illness pays compensation for each of the days missed recovers, then they are responsible for making up the days they have missed. Otherwise, it would be as if they had paid money to rid themselves of the responsibility to perform the acts of worship, which is neither right nor acceptable. This is only admissible in case of absolute necessity. If the person who cannot fast is also too poor to pay the compensation, then they have no responsibility to do so. Such people must repent for their past sins, remember Allah, and ask for His forgiveness.

# Maxims About Fasting

## Some sayings of the Prophet about fasting

- Fasting is a worship that has been entrusted to you. Therefore, all of you must protect the trust delivered by Allah and must not lose it.
- Do you know what is better than fasting, charity, and prayer? It is making peace among people, as quarrels and bad feelings destroy humanity.
- Enduring hunger and thirst is not fasting. Fasting is refraining from obscene talk, bad contacts, the yoke of carnal desire, and evil actions.
- Whoever amongst you is able to marry then let them do so, for marriage better protects the eyes from looking at the unlawful, better guards against fornication. But whoever is not able to marry then let them fast, for it breaks the feeling of lust.
- The invocation of three persons is not returned unanswered: The invocation of the fasting per-

son, the invocation of the traveler, and the invocation of the oppressed.

## Words of wisdom about fasting

- There are seven things in which there is no goodness: performing prayers without reverence, fasting without refraining from unnecessary things, reciting the Qur'an fast and carelessly, worship that does not prevent sins, prosperity that does not lead to generosity, friendship without sincerity, and supplication without cordiality. (Ali ibn Abu Talib)
- If I fast for life, spend the nights in worship without any sleep, give away all my possessions in the cause of Allah, but do not have any affection for those who submit to Allah and hate those who rebel against Allah, I will find no goodness in any of my acts of worship. (Abdullah ibn Umar)
- If worship were a bird, certainly fasting and daily prayers would be its wings. (Yahya ibn Mu'adh)
- The person who fasts without hunger is the person who eats and drinks but protects the limbs against sins. The person who does not fast while fasting, on the other hand, is the one who does not eat or drink but does not protect the limbs against sins. (Imam Ghazali)

- One of the manners of fasting is to stay awake during the day in order to feel hunger, thirst, and feebleness. (Imam Ghazali)
- Abstaining from food and drink without refraining from committing sins is like seemingly making ablution but failing to complete it, wiping the limbs three times with wet hands without washing them up. (Imam Ghazali)
- Prayers will take you half of the way. Fasting takes you to the door of the Sovereign. As for charity, it takes you to the presence of the Sovereign. (Umar ibn Abdulaziz)
- Fasting becomes a key to thanksgiving, which is the real duty of human beings in many respects. (Bediüzzaman Said Nursi)
- Fasting in the month of Ramadan is a key to real, genuine, great, and common thanksgiving. (Bediüzzaman Said Nursi)
- Fasting in the month of Ramadan deals a blow directly against the arrogance of the carnal soul and smashes it. It makes the desperation, weakness, and destitution of humanity visible. It makes them remember that they are the servant. (Bediüzzaman Said Nursi)
- In Holy Ramadan every soul from the most prosperous to the poorest understands that they are not the owner but the owned; not the master but

the servant. Seeing that they cannot do even the easiest thing without being ordered to and that they cannot reach for water, their pseudo lordship is demolished. They remember that they are the servant and thank Allah; this is their true obligation. (Bediüzzaman Said Nursi)

- The most perfect fasting is that which makes all senses and faculties, such as the eyes, ears, heart, imagination, and intellect fast as the stomach does. That is, human beings must also refrain from prohibited deeds and useless things that do not concern them and which lead each of their organs in its own special way of worshipping. (Bediüzzaman Said Nursi)
- Fasting is both a physical and spiritual diet, which is the most important kind of medicine. (Bediüzzaman Said Nursi)
- The medicine for impatience and intolerance, things that increase the calamities of people, is fasting. (Bediüzzaman Said Nursi)
- People who do not fast are suppressed by the weight of their body and they never attain a complete spiritual maturity. (M. Fethullah Gülen)
- Fasting is a most excellent worship, one in which the sense of fidelity is manifested. (M. Fethullah Gülen)

- With fasting, human beings build a barrier against the evil thoughts that their carnal self whispers to them . . . then they take the bridles into their hand and try to direct their carnal self. (M. Fethullah Gülen)
- Another meaning of fasting is the asceticism of soul and mortification of flesh. (M. Fethullah Gülen)
- Fasting teaches human beings to always comply with and protect the things entrusted to them either manifestly or in secret. (M. Fethullah Gülen)

# Appendix

## The Effect of Fasting upon Human Health

Body Weight: The effect of fasting upon body weight is demonstrated in the following table. The unit of measurement used in the study is one Ritl, corresponding to 410 g. The figures in the table have been converted to kilograms.

| | Before Ramadan | During Ramadan | | | After Ramadan |
|---|---|---|---|---|---|
| | a | b | c | d | e |
| Non-fasting volunteer | 58.22 | 57.4 | 57.4 | 58.22 | 58.22 |
| Fasting volunteers (average) | 50.02 | 50.02 | 49.61 | 48.79 | 49.61 |
| Fasting pregnant woman | 43.46 | 43.46 | 44.28 | 45.1 | 47.97 |

Blood sugar rate: The changes in the blood sugar rate observed during the experiment are detailed in the table below. The unit of measurement was taken as mg/200mm3.

| | Before Ramadan | During Ramadan | | | After Ramadan |
|---|---|---|---|---|---|
| | a | b | c | d | e |
| Non-fasting volunteer | 92 | 87 | 90 | 88 | 93 |
| Fasting volunteers (average) | 88 | 80 | 80 | 84 | 86 |
| Fasting pregnant woman | 88 | 84 | 72 | 68 | 84 |

a = Pre-Ramadan data

b, c, d = Data of the first, the tenth, and the last days of Ramadan

e = Data recorded one month after Ramadan

# Bibliography


Abd ibn Humayd, Musnad, Cairo: Maktab al-Sunna, 1988.

Abdul Fattah Tabbara, İlmin Işığında İslâmiyet (Islam in the Light of Science), trans. Mustafa Öz, Istanbul: Kalem Yayınları, 1977.

______________, Ruh al-Din al-Islami, Beirut, 1977.

Abdur Razzaq Nawfal, Islâm ve Modern Ilim (Islam and Modern Science), Istanbul: Sönmez Yayınları, 1970.

Abu Dawud, Sulayman ibn Ash'as al-Sijistani, as-Sunan, Beirut: Dar al-Jinan, 1988.

Ahmad ibn Hanbal, Musnad, Beirut, 1969.

Ahmet Kahraman, Dinler Tarihi (History of Religions), Istanbul, 1975.

Ali al-Qariyy, Mirqat al-Mafatih, Cairo: Matbaat al-Maymaniyya, 1891.

Ali al-Muttaqi, Alaaddin al-Muttaqi ibn Husamaddin al-Hindi, Kanz al-Ummal fi Sunan al-Aqwali wa al-Af'al, Beirut: Muassasat ar-Risala, 1989.

Alparslan Özyazıcı, Din ve Bilimin Işığında Oruç ve Sağlık (Fasting and Health in the Light of Religion and Science), Ankara: Diyanet Işleri Başkanlığı Yayınları, 2004.

Ayni, al-Binaya fi Sharh al-Hidaya, Beirut: Dar al-Fikr, 1980.

______________, Umdat al-Qaari, Cairo: Sharika Maktaba wa Matbaa al-Halabi, 1972.

Bediüzzaman Said Nursi, Risale-i Nur Külliyatı, Vols I–II, Istanbul: Nesil Yayınları, 2002.

Bayhaqi, Sunan al-Kubra, Khaydarabad: Dairat al-Maarif al-Osmaniyya, 1925.

Bukhari, Muhammad ibn Ismail; al-Jami al-Sahih, Beirut: Dar al-Kutub al-Ilmiyya, 1994.

Buhuti, Kashshaf al-Qina, Beirut: Dar al-Fikr, 1982.

Celal Kırca, Kur'an-ı Kerim'de Fen Bilimleri (Sciences in the Qur'an), Istanbul: Marifet Yayınları, 1984.

Darimi, Sunan al-Darimi, Beirut: Dar al-Kitab al-Arabi, 1987.

Dasuki, Hashiya ala al-Sharh al-Kabir, Dar al-Kutub al-Arabiyya, 1912.

Daylami, Firdaws, Vol. II.

Elmalılı Hamdi Yazır, Hak Dini Kur'an Dili (Language of the Qur'an, the True Faith), Istanbul: Eser Neşriyat, 1978.

Imam Ghazali, Ihya Ulum al-Din, Istanbul: Arslan Yayınları, 1993.

Hafid ibn Rushd, Bidayat al-Mujtahid, Cairo: Maktabat al-Tijarat al-Kubra, undated.

Hakim an-Nisaburi, Mustadrak, Beirut: Dar al-Kutub al-Ilmiyya, 1990.

Haluk Nurbaki, Kur'an-ı Kerim'den Ayetler ve İlmi Gerçekler (Verses from the Qur'an and Scientific Facts), Ankara: Türkiye Diyanet Vakfı, 1993.

Mawsuat al-Fiqhiyya, Kuwait: Wazarat al-Awqaf wa al-Shuun al-Islamiyya, 1983.

Ibn Abdulbarr, al-Tamhid, Titvan: Wazarat al-Awqaf wa al-Shuun al-Islamiyya, 1974.

Ibn Abidin, Radd al-Mukhtar, Cairo: Sharika Maktaba wa Matbaa Mustafa al-Babi al-Halabi, 1966.

Ibn Abi Shayba, Musannaf, Khaydarabad: Matbaat al-Aziziya, 1966.

Ibn Qudama, Mughni, Riyadh: Maktabat al-Jumhuriyyat al-Arabiyya, undated.

Ibn Maja, Muhammad ibn Yazid al-Qazwini, Sunan, Beirut: Dar al-Kutub al-Ilmiyya, undated.

Ibrahim Canan, Hazreti Peygamber'in Sünnetinde Terbiye (Education in the Teachings of the Prophet), Istanbul: Cihan Yayınları, 1982.

Imam Malik, Malik ibn Anas al-Asbahi, al-Muwatta, Cairo: Dar al-Hadith, 1993.

Imam Rabbani, Mektubat-ı Rabbani, Istanbul: Cümle Yayınları, 1986.

Kandahlawi, Awjaz al-Masalik ila Muwatta Malik, Beirut: Dar al-Fikr, 1989.

Kasani, Badai al-Sanai, Beirut: Dar al-Kutub al-Ilmiyya, 1997.

M. Fuad Abdulbaqi, Mujam al-Mufahras li Alfaz al-Qur'an, Cairo: Dar al-Hadith, 1988.

Mehmet Demirci, İbadetlerin İç Anlamı (The Inner Meaning of Worships), Ankara: Tasavvuf Dergisi, Issue 3, 2000.

Mehmet Taplamacıoğlu, Karşılaştırmalı Dinler Tarihi (Compared History of Religions), Ankara: Güneş Matbaacılık, 1966.

Mawsili, al-Ikhtiyar, Istanbul: Çağrı Yayınları, 1987.

Mundhiri, al-Targhib wa al-Tarhib, Istanbul: Pamuk Yayınları, undated.

Muslim, Abu al-Husayn al-Hajjaj al-Nisaburi; Sahih al-Muslim, Beirut: Dar al-Ihya al-Turath al-Arabi, undated.

Nadwi, Dört Rükun (The Four Pillars), Istanbul: Nehir Yayınları, undated.

Nasai, Abu Abdurrahman Ahmad ibn Shuayb an-Nasai, al-Sunan al-Kubra, (edition critique by Sulayman al-Bundari and Sayyid Hasan, Beirut: 1991.

Nawawi, Majmu, Beirut: Dar al-Fikr, undated.

Ömer Faruk Harman, Metin, Muhteva ve Kaynak Açısından Yahudi Kutsal Kitapları, (Jewish Scriptures from the Aspect of Texture, Content, and Source), Istanbul, 1988.

Said Hawwa, al-Islam, Cairo: Dar al-Salaam,1988.

Sarahsi, Mabsut, Cairo: Matbaat al-Saada, 1912.

Seyfettin Yazıcı, Ramazan ve Oruç (Ramadan and Fasting), Ankara: Diyanet Yayınları, 1997.

Shadid Athar et al., Health and Ramadan, First International Congress, Casablanca, 1994.

Shihabuddin al-Ramli, Nihayat al-Muhtaj, Beirut: Dar al-Fikr, 1984.

Tabarani, Mujam al-Awsat, Riyadh: Maktabat al-Maarif, 1985.

______________, Mujam al-Kabir, Riyadh: Maktabat al-Maarif, 1985.

Tahir Olgun, Müslümanlıkta Ibadet Tarihi (History of Worship in Islam), Istanbul, 1946.

Tahsin Feyizli, İslam'da ve Diğer İnanç Sistemlerinde Oruç-Kurban (Fasting and Sacrifice in Islam and Other Belief Systems), Istanbul: Milli Eğitim Bakanlığı Yayınları, undated.

Tahanawi, Ila al-Sunan, Idarat al-Qur'an wa al-Ulum, Karachi, 1995.

Tirmidhi, Abu Isa Muhammad ibn Isa, Jami al-Sahih, Beirut, undated.

Zaylai, Nasb al-Raya, Maktabat al-Islamiyya, 1973.

Zuhayli, Fiqh al-Islami wa Adillatuhu, Damascus: Dar al-Fikr, 1985.

Made in the USA
Monee, IL
21 March 2023

30302083R00121